Uncrowned Queens:

African American Women Community Builders of Western New York

Volume II

Written and Edited by

Barbara Seals Nevergold, Ph.D.
Peggy Brooks-Bertram, Dr. PH, Ph.D.

Foreword by
Levirn Hill, Editor
A History of the Underground Railroad in Howard County Maryland
Black American Colleges and Universities

Cover Art by Dennis A. Bertram
After a photograph by Margie D. Johnson
of Peggy Brooks and Audrey Brooks
in the 1600 block of Barnes Street
Baltimore, Maryland

Cover Design and Book Layout by Lisa C. Francescone

Address all inquires to:
Uncrowned Queens Institute for Research and Education on Women, Inc.
984 Parkside Avenue
Buffalo, New York 14216

E-mail comments or questions to
uncrownedqueens@buffalo.com

Printed in Buffalo, New York by Petit Printing
ISBN: 0-9722977-1-5

Visit our Web site
Uncrowned Queens: African American Women
Community Builders of Western New York
http://wings.buffalo.edu/uncrownedqueens

To my sister, Audrey Brooks, who posed with me in the photo that is the cover to this second volume, more than fifty years ago in the 1600 block of Barnes Street, in an East Baltimore slum from which few escaped unscarred. I love you Audrey. The photo was taken by my sister Margie, now deceased. We still miss her. Artist Dennis Bertram breathed new life into the photo, worked wonders with his artists' palette and produced this cover.

Peggy Brooks-Bertram

To my "big" sister, Mildred Irene Seals Wiggins, whose quiet manner, gracious demeanor, and loving character belie her inner strength and ability to be an ever-present, steadfast source of support for her family. Her love and encouragement of me are deeply appreciated and returned in a measure that, hopefully, equates in some way to hers. I love you, Millie.

Barbara Ann Seals Nevergold

Table of Contents

Acknowledgements

Like Volume I, Uncrowned Queens: *African American Women Community Builders of Western New York,* Volume II, has also been a labor of love and is a continuation of the first book project that originated from the Uncrowned Queens Web site at http://wings.buffalo.edu/uncrownedqueens. This volume was created in response to numerous requests to continue this regional effort to celebrate the accomplishments of African American women in Western New York. Four years later and more than six hundred women on the Web site, we are immensely proud at the outcome of this continuing effort to document the history of African American women and their contributions to the building of Western New York.

During the course of 2003, we continued to receive the support and well wishes of an entire community as reflected in partnerships as diverse as the women represented herein. The list is long and includes notable community organizations, church groups, businesses, and private individuals. Most notable of the partnerships is Tops Friendly Markets; Buffalo Teachers Federation; Buffalo Museum of Science; Mary B. Talbert Civic and Cultural Club; Iota Phi Lambda Sorority, Inc.; Alpha Kappa Alpha Sorority, Inc.; Kaleida Health; the Buffalo and Erie County Historical Society; *The Buffalo Challenger;* the *Buffalo Criterion;* St. Philip's Episcopal Church; the Afro-American Historical Association of the Niagara Frontier, Inc.; Buffalo and Erie County Public Library; the Buffalo Urban League; the Michigan Avenue Preservation Corporation; Forest Lawn Group; YWCA of Western New York; Erie County Chapter of The Links, Incorporated; Chris Del Prince of Life Styles; Robert Doyle, State Farm Insurance; Alpha Beta Sigma Sorority; Niagara Falls Housing Authority, Inc.; Niagara Falls Chapter of The Links, Incorporated; the Pitt-Douglass Club; Rochester Chapter of The Links, Incorporated; About Time Magazine; Niagara Falls, Ontario Black History Society; Institute for African Studies, Russian Academy of Sciences; St. John Baptist Church; and the Reverend Dr. Bennett W. Smith Family Life Center.

We also acknowledge the partnership of the *Uncrowned Queens Institute* with the University at Buffalo including the Office of the President; Office of the Provost; the University at Buffalo Libraries;

Departments of African American Studies and Women's Studies; the Women and Gender Institute; Cora P. Maloney College; the Educational Opportunity Center; and the Center for Applied Technologies in Education. Individuals providing support are numerous and extremely important to us and we cannot begin to name each one individually for fear that we would run the risk of omitting someone. Nonetheless, our heartfelt thanks are extended to the individuals in Western New York as well as our families and friends for assisting us on this very important journey.

Barbara A. Seals Nevergold, Ph.D.
Peggy A. Brooks-Bertram, Dr. P.H., Ph.D.

Foreword

As editor of *A History of the Underground Railroad in Howard County Maryland* and *Black American Colleges and Universities,* I am honored to write the foreword for Volume II of *Uncrowned Queens: African American Women Community Builders of Western New York.* The first book, Volume I, grew from responses to the internationally acclaimed and award winning Web site at http://wings.buffalo.edu/uncrownedqueens and the urgings of the African American community across the region and the country. Through online inquiries, sometimes reaching a total of 35,000 monthly, and other communications, the community's response to this work was tremendous. and Volume I, made an enormous contribution to the burgeoning field of African American women's history. The creation of the "techno-pedia," utilizing web-based technology and the literary genre of biographical sketches accompanied by photographs, is the only African American women's regional history project of its kind. This earlier volume celebrated the range of experiences and achievements of black women in the Western New York area and is a historical template for regional historians.

Volume II is a continuation of this unique effort and documents the activities and contributions of another one hundred women. The narratives reveal a plethora of activities documenting African American women's lives in their homes, businesses, churches and community-based organizations and academic institutions. Many uncrowned queens started in very humble beginnings in Western New York and went on to distinguish themselves in various fields including literature. Volume II includes distinguished women authors such as Connie Rose Porter, author of the world-famous *Addy* books and *Imani All Mine*; Lucille Clifton, Pulitzer Prize nominee and Poet Laureate of the State of Maryland; Shirley Hailstock, award winning novelist and first black President of the Romance Writers of America; Virginia DeBerry, best selling author of *Tryin' to Sleep in the Bed You Made;* Karla Holloway author of numerous books including *Passed On: African American Mourning Stories,* and others.

At the same time, Volume II succeeds at what was the initial and continuing goal of the *Uncrowned Queens Institute*: recognition of the not so famous and previously unrecognized, but no less important and indispensable stalwarts in the maintenance and sustainability of the Western New York African American community. These include African American women from the turn of the century such as Bertha Amos, a church builder; Mary E. Wood, YWCA Executive Director; Pauline Winifred Huff Byrd, organist; Clara L. Payne a member of the Progressive Club host committee for the Pan American Exposition of 1901, and more contemporary women such as Doris Jones, founder of the Niagara Improvement Association of Niagara County; Katherine Kirkland owner of Kirkland's Turquoise Diner and many more.

The women in Volume II also represent many Western New York communities including Buffalo, Rochester, Lackawanna, Niagara Falls and Depew, New York. Volume II also reaches across the disciplines to include Women's Studies, African American Studies as well as American History. It includes black women in the fields of art, business, education, government, law, literature, social sciences, health, performing arts and science. The uniqueness of the volume is that it is written by the community for the community as a direct response to the community's wishes. Some women may never have shared their activities but they were encouraged by friends, family and colleagues to share their achievements not just with the Western New York community but also with the world.

One is also struck with the number of church organizations, especially the diversity of religious denominations, women's participation in all levels of their communities including corporate board membership/leadership, community-based volunteerism, business ownership and the longevity and dearth of participation in sororities and historically black club women enterprises. Whatever the circumstances of their lives, black women have a rich and varied history that has been only partially told. The Uncrowned Queens project helps to address this omission and create another venue by which the regional histories of African American women can come into the consciousness of students, educators, scholar/historians and the uncrowned queens themselves.

In essence, Volume II is like a pebble tossed on the historical waters, its ripple effects are far-reaching. Already other states have expressed interest in replicating the entire Uncrowned Queens project, and writing their regional histories in similar volumes. The task of gathering these histories and adding them to the vast regional history of Western New York via the Internet is a tremendous undertaking that should be replicated across the country.

I am currently identifying opportunities to replicate the project in the State of Maryland. The first replication is currently taking place in the State of Oklahoma. Truly, this volume is a community's unabashed celebration of itself and it's about time.

Levirn Hill
Editor, Librarian, Former Western New Yorker

Preface

"Sisterhood" depicts the early age at which the concept of sisterhood is developed in the African American community. The decision to use this painting, adapted by artist Dennis Bertram, from a childhood photo of sisters Peggy and Audrey Brooks, is grounded in the belief that ideas of sisterhood in the African American community begin early and endure forever. The biographies in the Uncrowned Queens digital techno-pedia, on line at http://wings.buffalo.edu/uncrownedqueens reveal not only longevity of sisterhood but also the power of this belief to grow, nurture, and sustain the African American community.

Sisterhood is timeless with ancient African beginnings. In the African American community sisterhood is deeply revered, unspoken yet socially required, and not without its own special pains—mostly from remnants of a fractured past history of slavery and Jim Crow. Nonetheless, sisterhood is endless.

The women honored in this volume, as in Vol. I, constitute a family of sisters, some dating from the late nineteenth century until the present day. While each makes her own distinct contribution, their strength is in numbers as they weave together the threads of myriad African American families–many from the post-slavery South–into sustainable Western New York communities. These sisters were indefatigable. They created communities under-girded by their sacred institutions, the Church, the institutions of knowledge, the public schools, colleges and universities, and social organizations, e.g., sororities and fraternities, that both sustain and bind them to sisterhood. They leave an extraordinary legacy for their children and their children's children. We are honored to have the privilege of documenting the "Sisterhood" of African American women of Western New York.

About the Poem

The inspiration for the title Uncrowned Queens was derived from the poem, "America's Uncrowned Queens," written by Drusilla Dunjee Houston more than three quarters of a century ago. For more than four decades, Houston wrote voluminously across several genres including poetry, elegy, editorials, essays, and historical texts. She contributed enormously to building the African American community in Oklahoma where she was a giant among black clubwomen of her era. Regrettably, her achievements went unheralded and Houston became one of the toiling "uncrowned queens" about whom she wrote. In recognition of her achievements throughout her life, we dedicate this book in her memory.

America's Uncrowned Queens:
Dedicated to the Heroic, Toiling Black Woman
by Drusilla Dunjee Houston

The Black Dispatch, October 26, 1917
Courtesy of the Oklahoma Historical Society

'Neath a weary load upon dusky head,
Upon American streets is the tread
Of an uncrowned type of heroine,
Their labors untrumpeted and unseen.
It to her helpmate, life chance is denied
With undaunted courage, she stems the tide,
Meets some of homes needs, help make it fair;
That he may find a kingship there.

When manhood is shackled, into its place
Nature oft forces a courageous race
Of women, who with heroic spirit,
Stamp within unborn children the merit
Denied their fathers. For what man's disdain
Keeps from one generation, the next will gain.

We see them in rain, in cold and the heat,
As they pass us with patient, toil worn feet.
Behind some great universities wall
It is the boy or girl for whom she gives all
Sometimes the more sacrificial her fire
The less we praise it, the more we require.

Whipped with the lash, until the reddened stain,
Of her life blood ran from opening vein,
In slavery's hour, this type was true
To virtue. Today life's way they pursue
As heroically. No scorn or slight
Can change her ideals, she sees aright;
That duty done, in higher worlds will mean
That she will be more than an uncrowned queen.

Introduction

Volume I grew out of the *Uncrowned Queens Institute* Web site, http://wings.buffalo.edu/uncrownedqueens, that was constructed to contribute to Buffalo's 2001 commemoration of the 1901 Pan American Exposition and to celebrate the contributions of African American women to the Exposition. The initial, as well as continuing goal, for the Web site is to identify 1,901 African American women whom helped to build the Western New York community over the past century. To date we have identified more than 600 women, most of who are on the Web site with photographs and biographical sketches.

Volume II is second in a series of volumes and recognizes an additional 100 African American women. This volume is still rooted in the idea of the accomplishments of African American women over the past century as well as the type and longevity of the institutions they built to sustain their community and, indeed, the entire Western New York community. Utilizing the literary genre of the biographical sketch, the book provides a glimpse at the contributions of these community builders. A photograph accompanies each sketch allowing the reader to connect extraordinary activities with a face. The biographical sketches have myriad authors including the Uncrowned Queens themselves, family members, friends, and interested others. Thus, it is not a book of self-adoration but rather a reflection of what a community thinks about itself.

A close review of the information reveals much about African American women's need, love, and appreciation for the entire community. One of the most anticipated and important characteristic of these women is their role in the building and maintenance of a broad Church community. Analysis of the number and diversity of churches represented in these biographies is impressive. For instance, these 100 women represent affiliations with nearly sixty different churches with diverse denominations. And, it is clear, as demonstrated in Volume I, that the Church figures prominently in the lives of these women. These biographies reveal that much of the work of the African American community is conducted through the myriad activities of these women in their churches. For instance, they utilize their educational achievements and corporate skills gained outside of the church to initiate faith-based community outreach and establish church-related businesses and educational entities. Their efforts are evident in the volume of faith-based initiatives such as charter schools; health-related facilities; after school educational programs for young people; recreational centers; and special ministries to support the sick, shut-ins, nursing home residents, the incarcerated, the homeless, and others. It can be surmised that this level of association/identification with the church also contributes significantly to the financial viability of the church. Of particular note is the rise of unique faith-based initiatives in health, e.g., the St. John Baptist Church, African American Hospice facility. In this instance, a religious institution works collaboratively with a major health care corporate entity to build the first African American Hospice facility in the country. Women with skills in public health, nursing, medicine and health care administration constitute the bulk of the committee that spearheads this groundbreaking activity. In the area of nursing care for the elderly, other women were instrumental in establishing the first African American nursing home in the area, e.g., Grace Manor Nursing Home.

African American women community builders also play critical roles in their churches in other areas, e.g., directing Christian education programs; conducting local and foreign missionary work; providing nursing services for church pastors as well as parishioners; implementing projects to clothe, feed and educate the less fortunate; maintaining and sustaining church history through record keeping and other documentation and initiating and maintaining specific church ministries, e.g., health, education, and others. Some of these women are identified early on as evangelists who engaged in the opening of "new mission fields" that contribute to the growth and development of the church in the community. There are also records of African American women opening their homes to the needy or purchasing church land to build and preach in their own churches. In some instances, these women have utilized their skills as administrators to orchestrate their churches to serve as delegate agencies for major federal projects benefiting poor children and their families, e.g., Head Start.

Uncrowned Queens also engage in numerous activities within the governing structure of their churches, taking a lead role in spiritual as well as secular activities. They serve as Deacons and Trustees who manage the social, political and economic affairs of the church.

Through their musical skills either individually, in choral groups, as instrumentalists, e.g., piano, organ and drums, or choir directors, they extend the reach of the church, maintain musical traditions and enhance the opportunity for community-wide celebration and fellowship. Thus, African American women and their support of the African American church is a powerful force in the African American community.

Numerous women provide other legacies through their writings. The biographical sketches in this volume reflect a rich collection of prolific writers whose works cross numerous genres, including poetry, screenplays, essays, epics, historical texts, documentaries in sculpture and photographs, and still others who have produced mountains of other works, albeit much of it unpublished. A few of the many writers include Shirley Hailstock, Patrice Cathey, April Coley, Connie Porter, Virginia DeBerry, Karla Holloway, Samada Nur, and others. This rich literary legacy is not only a reflection of the unique talents of these women, but is also a testament to their abilities to manage many tasks simultaneously, e.g., many held 2 jobs, managed families, sought higher education and supported their Churches while simultaneously producing volumes of written materials.

Also striking is the participation of these Uncrowned Queens on major corporate Boards of Directors across the country including Imagining America; Arts and Scholars in Public Life; North Carolina Humanities Council; National Black Herstory Task Force; Fordham University Press; Inter-University Seminar on Armed Forces and Society and others. Other corporate structures include Greenwall Foundation; World Federation of Methodist Women; National Board, NAACP; General Board of Church and Society; American Cancer Society; National Association for Social Workers; National Conference for Community and Justice; National Association of Young Women Executives; Energy East Corporation and others. In Buffalo and closer environs, Uncrowned Queens serve on the boards of numerous organizations including the Rochester Area Foundation; Blue Cross Blue Shield of Rochester; Niagara Frontier Transportation Authority; Leadership Buffalo; Buffalo Philharmonic Orchestra Society; Rochester School for the Deaf; Monroe County Sports Commission; United Way; Kaleida Health; King Urban Life Center; Erie County Mental Health Association; St. Philip's Community Center; Buffalo

Federation of Neighborhood Centers; Inc., the Buffalo and Erie County Historical Society and the Langston Hughes Cultural Institute.

Many serve on University and College Boards of Directors and Boards of Trustees including the University of Rochester; Monroe Community College; Robert Wesleyan College; Medaille College; Buffalo State College Foundation; Board of Regents; Canisius College; Bennett College and St. Bonaventure University. Other Boards of Directors connected with higher education include the New York State Education Department Board of Regents; Canisius College Alumnae Association; the College Board Advisory Council; Princeton University Advisory Council for the Program in the Study of Women and Gender and others. In addition to the diversity of boards of corporate structures on which African American women serve, nearly one hundred other educational/historical/cultural/organizations, which are the backbone of the community, are represented in their biographies.

Uncrowned Queens are also world travelers many of whom studied abroad on the African continent, in Europe, China, Japan, Canada and South America. Together they present a vast array of talents directed either singly or in concert, to the development, growth and sustainability of the Western New York community.

The *Uncrowned Queens Institute* continues to be an instrument to bring community groups together. Continuing partnerships and networks with non-profit organizations, community self-help groups, government agencies, businesses, educational institutions, and the media, demonstrate the tremendous potential of this project to garner widespread, diverse support. This networking has resulted in numerous community-wide Uncrowned Queens events, most notably the official launch of the Web site in February 2001; the first annual conference; *Lifting as They Climbed: A Century of Community Building* 1901-2001, held November 9 - 11, 2001; the second annual conference, *Commemorating our Past, Preserving our Present and Sustaining our Future,* held November 15-16, 2002 and the 2003 award notification from the Oklahoma Capitol Complex and Centennial Commemoration Commission that the Uncrowned Queens Project was placed on the Master Plan of the Oklahoma Centennial Celebration for 2007 and would be replicated in the State of Oklahoma.

Given the utility and diversity of the Web site, the widespread dissemination of information and education about the Institute and its programs, the question may be posed, 'Why is this book necessary?' A goal of the *Uncrowned Queens Institute* is to provide educational materials to enhance the teaching of local history. This second book is in keeping with that original goal. Further, numerous requests from the African American community to provide a "hard copy" of the "Queens" on the Web site makes this book necessary. In response to these requests, we decided to publish a series of books that would be useful for individuals who are not yet computer literate, but who would like to have a book on the Uncrowned Queens for their private libraries.

Like Volume I, this volume contains the bio-sketches of 100 women, all randomly selected. These women are grouped according to broad categories such as Artists, Authors, Business, Community Organizations, Education, Health, Historians, Media, and Politics and Government. Early in this project, we were amazed at the variety of interests and achievements of the Uncrowned Queens making it difficult to place individual women in the various categories. We took the liberty of making assignments that reflected the broadest possible angle for individual women. Further, Our goal was to focus the spotlight on those areas for which individual women were active, but for which they did not necessarily receive attention. Thus we hoped to illuminate our "queens" in very different lights. We trust we succeeded in that goal.

Uncrowned Queens in the Arts

Patrice Cathey

Patrice Cathey is a native of Buffalo, New York. She is the daughter of the late Eulis M. Cathey, Sr., former Erie County Probation Officer and Mrs. Ruth H. Cathey, retired Buffalo Public School teacher and coach. She has one brother, Eulis Cathey, Jr. of New York City. She is a graduate of the Buffalo Seminary and received a certificate of Interior Design from John Robert Powers Career School. She has a B.A. in English, and a M.S. Ed. from Canisius College. Patrice is working towards a Ph.D. in Higher Education with an expected completion in 2005.

Patrice is an internationally recognized poet, performer, educator, and children's advocate. She began her career in education teaching in the Project Gift Program at St. John Baptist Church. Prior to her education career, Ms. Cathey owned Classique' Creations Interior Design Studio and participated in two Junior League Show Houses.

Patrice has founded numerous companies and organizations including Ethic and Etiquette, Poetically Speaking Poetry Workshops for Children and Onya Publishing. This unique publishing house specializes in poetry chatbooks and short stories. Patrice's publications include, *Sounds of Poetry,* and an anthology of select poets throughout the world entitled, *Friends I've Never Met, Heart of My Hands and Nubian Princess.*

As a performance poet Patrice reads her poetry with jazz accompaniment working with such notable jazz musicians as the late Al Tinney. Her many awards include, International Society of Poetry Yearly Award, The Poetry Woman of the Year Award, and the Buffalo Seminary 2002 Distinguished Alumnae Award. Her professional organization memberships include, AEEE, National Black Educators, Women in Higher Education, The National Association of University Women, and numerous poetry societies.

Patrice is the proud mother of three sons, Jonathan Eulis, Stephan James, and Patrick Jason Barr.

Valeria Cray-Dihaan

The eldest of eight siblings, Valeria Annette Cray was born in West Palm Beach, Florida, to Leadley and Annie Mae Sherrod Cray. Her mother encouraged her artistically and told her, "When God created artists, they were special people with a special gift of seeing, hearing and feeling things differently than others." Leadley Cray, Valeria's father, was a self-taught auto mechanic, who learned through practical experience.

Both Leadley and Annie Mae felt that education was the most important part of their children's life. After losing her mother, Valeria and her siblings were reared by their grandmother and later their aunt, Ruby Sherrod Jones. Valeria's artistic excellence was recognized and encouraged by her family. Today, Valeria is a sculptor working in the mediums of ceramics, copper, aluminum, acetate, jute, textiles, plexi-glass and wood. She was nurtured early in life by the example and inspiration gained from her parents as well as other family members.

She holds a Bachelor of Fine Arts degree from the University of Buffalo and a Masters of Fine Arts degree from Pratt Institute, New York. While studying and teaching art with the Aztec Indians in the mountains of Tespostlan, Mexico, she assisted with the construction and organization of schools in the area. Cray-Dihaan also studied Jamaican art and culture. *Tension, Texture, and Design: The Soul of an Artist* is an exhibit of her latest work incorporating copper, stainless steel, acetate, plexi-glass and brass.

Valeria is a social activist and is president and founding member of the community based organization, 50 Women with a Vision, a major community project centered around the restoration of the Apollo Theater and other community projects on Jefferson Avenue in Buffalo.

Valeria is also a businesswoman and owns and operates East Wind, a salon specializing in hair loss and hair attachments. She is married to Sylvester Dihaan. Her son Hiram is also a visual artist whose artistic growth Valeria encourages.

Dodo Greene

Her birth name is Dorthea Hawkins, but she has been known as Dodo since she was a teenager. A Buffalo native, Dorthea "Dodo" Greene began singing at age 7 or 8 when she was chosen for recurrent appearances on the Buster Brown Shoes Amateur Hour radio program. She acknowledges being a frequent winner on the show and being rewarded with shoes for herself and her family. Dodo's talent was nurtured by a local music teacher and she became one of "Miss Margaret Scott's Personality Steppers." At age 77 she is still performing.

Dodo's family was a musical one. Her brothers were both musicians. James Hawkins was a drummer and Sonny Hawkins was a well-known local saxophone player. Her sister Alice was a dancer, but did not pursue a career in that field. Dodo's musical career did not begin in earnest until the late 40's. She said she got her first big singing job at the Club Moon-Glow, a nightclub at Michigan and William Street. She also sang at other local clubs on the eastside and the Cold Springs district, including The Musician's Club, The Buffalo Club, the Pine Grill, Mandy's and the Little Harlem.

In 1959 Dodo left Buffalo for New York City. In 1960 she joined Cab Calloway's Broadway production of "Cotton Comes to Harlem" at the Wintergarden Theater. Dodo became known at that time as the "buxom blues singer." It was also about this time that she perfected a Louis Armstrong imitation, including his trademark throaty growl and hanky and adopted her trademark bleached blonde hairstyle. She still performs the Armstrong tribute in her act to this day.

From her New York base, Dodo performed in the Catskill's resort area, New York City clubs and eventually toured Europe. She recorded an album with Blue Note Records and was the first female singer to record with that label. The album "My Hour of Need" is still available in CD form. She returned to Buffalo with plans to retire at age 60. However, friends convinced her to get back on stage and she began singing again at clubs such as the Blue Note and the Calumet Café.

Dodo is the proud mother of two sons. Sadly, both are deceased. She is proud of her sons and of their accomplishments and support for her career. She states that they are her inspiration and she feels their presence when she sings.

In 1997 Dodo was honored in Buffalo's Hall of Fame, along with music great Harold Arlen. Dodo Greene continues to perform weekends at the Anchor Bar. In a September 2002 interview with *The Buffalo News*, she described a recent performance; "I have a closing number that I sing, and I do a burlesque, *When You're Smiling*. I do it with a handkerchief and a little Satchmo. The other night, I was out of the building, and they were still applauding. I had to go back." Ms. Greene is a woman of great talent, boundless energy and an indomitable spirit who continues to "wow" her audiences.

Phoebe Parks

Phoebe (Lil) Parks was born in Raleigh, North Carolina to parents Professor Samuel and Tena Dunn. She attended Washington High School and St. Augustine College, where she met the Delaneys (of the Delaney Sister fame). Bishop Delaney confirmed her at St. Ambrose Episcopal Church in 1925, where she also sang in the choir.

Phoebe moved to New York City in 1930 after the death of her mother. She worked as manager of the cosmetic company of George W. Luft on Long Island. She won a week's performance at the Apollo Theater, and sang at the 101 Ranch, a nightclub in Harlem.

She moved to Buffalo in 1946 where she met and married the late James (Jerry) Parks. They raised six foster children. After retirement as a foster-parent, she worked for thirteen years as a supervisor of the meal program for seniors at Brent Manor. Lil is a member of St. Philip's Episcopal Church where she was a member of St. Joseph's Guild, Sunday School Teachers and Altar Guild. In addition, she is an active member of the William Emslie YMCA. She is well-known at the Colored Musician's Club. She formerly sang with the "New Sensational Seniors." At the age of 90, Lil still performs with a group,

The Bits-o-B'way at the Lancaster Opera House and various nursing homes and for private affairs.

Delores Ross

A life-long resident of Buffalo, Delores is the daughter of Terry Nathaniel and Virginia Neeley Winters. She received her formative education at school #75 and Hutchinson Central High School. She also earned a degree in business from Bryant and Stratton Business Institute.

Delores worked for more than 25 years as the Secretary for the Office of the Faculty and Professional Senate Office at the University at Buffalo. Upon her retirement, she received a certificate of appreciation for her numerous contributions to the University. While maintaining her position at the University at Buffalo, Delores also worked for the Buffalo Sewer Authority Board. She was the first Black woman to hold the post of secretary with the Authority.

Delores is a sought-after artist who specializes in portraits. Of her artistic talents, Delores notes that she is primarily self-taught and has never taken a class on anatomy. She has been drawing all of her life and has found it to be a true passion. She has painted portraits of most of the pastors in the city of Buffalo. In addition there are countless others who are blessed to have a Delores Ross original of themselves or of their loved ones.

Delores also has a long history of community activism and was a founding member of the Northern Region Black Political Caucus. She is very active in her church, First Shiloh Baptist Church, and is known as the "unofficial artist" of the church.

Delores is the proud mother of three sons, Doyle, Kevin, and Keith. Her family also includes her two sisters, Mildred and Mary.

Uncrowned Queen Authors

Lucille Clifton

Lucille Clifton was born Lucille Sayles in Buffalo, New York on June 27, 1936. She was raised in Depew, New York, a Buffalo suburb. After graduation from high school, she attended Howard University for three years before returning to New York State to complete undergraduate studies at the State University of New York College at Fredonia in 1955. She married Fred James Clifton in 1958.

She worked in several state and federal government positions before embarking on her literary career. She worked as a claims clerk in the New York State Division of Employment in Buffalo from 1958-1960. Following a move to the Washington, D.C. area in 1960 she was employed as a literature assistant in the Office of Education from 1960-1971.

Her first book, a collection of poetry entitled *Good Times,* was published in 1969. The New York Times identified it as one of the year's ten best books. In 1971, she was named poet-in-residence at Coppin State College, an Historically Black College in Baltimore, Maryland and held that position until 1974. During this period, she produced two further books of poetry, *Good News About the Earth* (1972) and *An Ordinary Woman* (1974). Ms. Clifton was named Poet Laureate of the state of Maryland in 1979.

Ms. Clifton was visiting writer at Columbia University School of the Arts and at George Washington University from 1982 to 1983. Afterwards she taught literature and creative writing at the University of California at Santa Cruz (1985) and then at St. Mary's College of Maryland. Ms. Clifton's later poetry collections include *Next; New Poems* (1987), *Quilting: Poem*s 1987-1990 (1991), and *The Terrible Stories* (1996). *Generations: A Memoir* (1976) is a prose piece celebrating her origins, and *Good Woman: Poems and a Memoir:* 1969-1980 (1987) collects some of her previously published verse.

She has also written for children. Her many children's books, written expressly for an African American audience in mind, include *All Us Come Cross the Water* (1973), *My Friend Jacob* (1980), and *Three Wishes* (1992). She also wrote an award-winning series of books featuring events in the life of Everett Anderson, a young black boy. These include *Some of the Days of Everett Anderson* (1970) and *Everett Anderson's Goodbye* (1983). Her children's books now total over 20.

Besides appearing in over 100 anthologies of poetry, Ms. Clifton has come to popular attention through television appearances on the *Today Show, Sunday Morning* with Charles Kuralt, *Nightline,* and Bill Moyers' series, *The Power of the Word.* She received Creative Writing Fellowships from the National Endowment for the Arts in 1970 and 1973, and a grant from The American Academy of Poets. She has received the Shelley Memorial Prize, the Charity Randall prize, the Shestack Prize from the American Poetry Review, and an Emmy Award. In 1988, she became the first author to have two books of poetry chosen as finalists for the Pulitzer Prize (*Good Woman* and *Next*).

Ms. Clifton has been the Distinguished Professor of Humanities at St. Mary's College of Maryland since 1991. She lives in Columbia, Maryland and has raised six children.

April Smith Coley

A native of Buffalo, April Smith Coley has called North Carolina home for many years. Leaving Buffalo in the late 70's because of the passing of her mother, the late Cottie B. Williams, she moved to North Carolina under the watchful eye of her grandmother Marrien M. Williams.

April is a graduate of North Carolina A&T State University where she received a B.S. in Business Administration-Marketing. She also studied at University of Maryland, and Winthrop College at Rock Hill, South Carolina.

She has served Allstate Insurance Company well in several management and leadership roles. The company has honored her with the esteemed Gold Medal Service Award, as well as several regional, and community service awards.

April has written several articles for the Charlotte Post. She was recognized by the Mecklenburg County Women's Commission for participating in the Women History Month Poetry Program. In 1999

April self published *Strivers Row*, a novel, which takes place initially in Buffalo, New York. April's poem Spiritual Nature was published by the National Library of Poetry in 1997. April is completing a non-fiction novel, and marketing two picture books for children.

Currently living in Raleigh, North Carolina, April is the Treasurer for the Montessori School of Raleigh, MPSA. She founded Circle of Friends America, Incorporated in February of 2002. Her commitment to her family and children are the driving force of her efforts. She serves as the marketing consultant on the Board of Directors for Amerikids, Incorporated.

April's husband is Duane O'Neil Coley. Duane also is an alumnus of North Carolina A&T State University, and has studied at the University of Maryland. They are the proud parents of Kinnidy Denise Coley and Zackary O'Neil Coley. Kinnidy and Zackary attend the Montessori School of Raleigh.

Virginia DeBerry

Virginia DeBerry, co-author of *Tryin' to Sleep in the Bed You Made, Far From the Tree,* and *Better Than I Know Myself* says "I'm proud to be a Buffalonian. I can't think of a better place to have grown up. This is where I learned the important things in life: family, friends, and community---the things I write about."

A product of the Buffalo Public Schools, Virginia attended schools 8, 74, 17, Fillmore Jr. High, and graduated from Bennett in 1967. Although she started college as an English major at Fisk University in Nashville, Tennessee, she completed her education at the University at Buffalo. "My parents were very influential in my education but I also must give credit to many of my teachers for nurturing my love of language and literature."

After college, Virginia began a career as an English teacher, where she taught at Genesee Humboldt, East, Lafayette and Seneca High Schools. After nearly ten years in the classroom, Virginia decided she needed a change. The opportunity to do something truly different, presented itself when a life-long friend, fellow Buffalonian, Lawrine

Childers, who worked at a New York modeling agency, convinced her to move downstate and try her hand at a brand new category in the fashion world: full figured modeling. Turning her life upside down, taking a chance and moving to New York proved to be a propitious decision and led to Virginia being frequently featured in catalogs, advertising and magazines, including Essence. She also appeared on TV programs like Today, Donahue, and Live with Regis and Kathie Lee. Choosing this unlikely fork in the road also led to meeting her writing partner, Donna Grant.

Although Virginia was a successful model, she retired after two years and became a booking agent, and later Agency Director, of BB/LW, an agency that represented large-size and petite models, which later became a part of the prestigious agency, Ford Models. At BB/LW, Virginia's background and experience as a teacher, led to the opportunity to become a spokeswoman for the large size fashion industry and for Hanes Hosiery. Virginia's career was the subject of articles in publications such as *US Magazine* and *Manhattan, Inc.* She was also interviewed on many local and nationally syndicated talk shows including PM Magazine, ESSENCE, the Television Program, and People are Talking.

After a stint as fashion editor of Great Dimensions newsletter, where she and Donna, who was celebrity focus editor, first worked together, Virginia went on to become the founding editor-in-chief of Maxima, a fashion and lifestyle magazine for the plus-size woman. Donna was the magazine's managing editor. When publication of Maxima ceased, Virginia and Donna realized that they had forged something beyond sisterhood. They had developed a working relationship they knew couldn't end. "So we decided it wouldn't!"

The two friends considered a few potential business opportunities, including starting another magazine. The two friends wondered if they could actually find a way to take advantage of what had been a first love for both of them... books. Once again, an unlikely decision turned out to be the right one. *Tryin' to Sleep in the Bed You Made* became a national bestseller and has sold more than half a million copies. It was the number one selling African American novel in 1997. *Tryin'* also won an Honor Award in Fiction from the Black Caucus of The American Library Association. *Far From the Tree* was released in 2000 and became a New York Times best seller. Virginia and Donna's newest novel, *Better Than I Know Myself* will be in bookstores in the Summer of 2004. "People often ask us how we can write fiction together. We don't know how or why it works and we've decided not to question it. It just works because it does."

Virginia now resides in Central New Jersey but is close to family and friends who still live in Buffalo. Her mother, Juanita DeBerry, is a retired Buffalo schoolteacher. Her brother, John L DeBerry III, MD, is a respected local surgeon and her sister Valerie DeBerry is an executive with Rich Products Corporation.

Lula Herring Gayles

Lula Lucritia Gayles Herring is the fourth oldest of seventeen sisters and brothers. They are the children of Edward Cato Gayles II and Lula Lucritia Adams Gayles. Lula is a native Buffalonian and is a published author, *These Women Better Get Smart*, playwright, *The Preacher Wo/man,* producer, actress and recording artist. Her musical contributions include the *Gayles Family Album and Stand America,* a song by Western New York musicians and singers. The proceeds of the latter will benefit the American Red Cross. Lula has also written the song, *It's not about me, it's all about Thee.*

Her other talents and training include: photographer, cosmetologist, certified social studies teacher, school administrator/ supervisor, school district administrator, evangelist, missionary, and foreign missionary and Sunday school teacher. Lula has been a Sunday school teacher since she was 15 years old. She acknowledges that she has completed reading the Bible in its entirety four times in this period.

Ms. Herring is Assistant Principal at Bennett High School in Buffalo. She has had many experiences in her life, but the most rewarding for her is when she can give and show love. "It is my philosophy that we are to achieve two things in this life and that is to love and be loved. Another philosophy is to be mentally, physically, and spiritually fit."

Lula is the wife of George D. Herring and mother of Bryan, David, Marc, Jennifer, and Linda. In addition, she is the grandmother of

Heather, Tiara, David, and Nathan. Her siblings include Eleanor, Rosa, Edward, Edna, George, Fred, Kenny, Pam, Alice, Marion, Ronald, Diane, Vivian, Gregg, Steven and Stanley. She is also the proud aunt of fifty-six nieces and nephews and fifty-two great-nieces and nephews.

Shirley Hailstock

Shirley Hailstock, best-selling, award-winning novelist, holds a bachelors degree in Chemistry from Howard University in Washington, D.C. and an MBA in Chemical Marketing from Fairleigh Dickinson University in Teaneck, NJ. Shirley's initial wish was to join the space program.

Whispers of Love, Shirley's debut novel, was published in September, 1994. The romantic suspense received critical acclaim from the Gothic Journal, Romantic Times Magazine, Affaire de Coeur Rendezvous and Booklist. *Whispers of Love,* winner of the HOLT Medallion from the Virginia Romance Writers, is now in its fourth printing and recently was optioned for a television movie of the week. *Clara's Promise,* Shirley's first historical romance, won the Utah Romance Writers Heart of the West Award. *White Diamonds,* (August 1996) was nominated for a Romantic Times Award as the Best Multicultural Romance of 1996. Additionally, Romantic Times presented Shirley with a Career Achievement Award and her novel, *Legacy,* received the Waldenbooks Award for Bestselling Multicultural Romance. *Legacy* was also recently listed as one of the 100 Greatest Romance Novels of the 20th Century. Her current book, *HIS 1-800 WIFE* is in bookstores now.

Shirley is a past president of the New Jersey Romance Writers. She has been a member of the Romance Writers of America since 1988 and served as Regional Director on the National Board for four years where she held positions of RITA Contest Chairperson, Golden Heart Contest Chairperson, Publicity Chairperson and Industry Statistic Chairperson. Shirley is also an officer of Women Writers of Color. She writes contemporary and historical romance and mainstream women's fiction.

Living in Central New Jersey with her two teenage children, Ashleigh and Christopher, Shirley has been an Adjunct Professor of Accounting at Rutgers University, New Brunswick campus and taught Novel Writing at Middlesex County College. Shirley was born in Buffalo, New York and is sister to another Uncrowned Queen, Wygenia Miles.

Karla Holloway

Dr. Karla FC Holloway is the Dean of Humanities and Social Sciences at Duke University where she holds the William R. Kenan Professorship of English and African American Studies. Professor Holloway is a graduate of the Buffalo Public Schools, Talladega College and Michigan State University—where she earned her PhD in English and Linguistics. Her professional career began as a teacher of eighth grade Language Arts at Clinton Jr. High School in Buffalo. She is the daughter of Claude D. and Ouida H. Clapp and the sister of Dr. Leslie Clapp Ezie.

Professor Holloway is the author of five books, including *Passed On: African American Mourning Stories; Codes of Conduct: Race, Ethics and the Color of Our Character; and Moorings and Metaphors: Figures of Culture and Gender in Black Women's Literature.* She has published numerous professional articles and reviews, provided guest commentary on National Public Radio and to magazines including *Emerge, The Crisis,* and *Black Issues in Higher Education,* and delivered lectures and keynote addresses across the United States as well as internationally—including England, France, Germany, and Turkey.

With past professorships at North Carolina State University, Western Michigan University and Old Dominion University, Dean Holloway is the first woman of color to hold a distinguished professorship at Duke University. As a member of its faculty, she has chaired the university's committee on Appointments, Promotions and Tenure that grants promotion and tenure to faculty of five of the university's schools, including Arts and Sciences, the School of Medicine, the Pratt School of Engineering, Divinity and the Fuqua

School of Business. She was the co-founder, in 1999, of the John Hope Franklin Center for International and Interdisciplinary Study at Duke, named to honor her friend and esteemed colleague, Dr. John Hope Franklin. In its inaugural years she assumed the role of co-director of the Center's Humanities Institute creating and overseeing its annual interdisciplinary seminar on race with foci on politics, religion, identity and globalization.

Following the publication of *Passed On,* and as a core faculty member of the Duke Institute on Care at the End of Life, Dr. Holloway has led national seminars and institutes on issues of end of life care, hospice and medical ethics involving African Americans. She is the featured speaker at the Institute's national seminar: "Crossing Over Jordan."

Her national board memberships have included The College Board's Advisory Council; the Greenwall Foundation's Advisory Board in Bioethics; Imagining America: Artists and Scholars in Public Life; the North Carolina Humanities Council and the Princeton University Advisory Council for the Program in the Study of Women and Gender. She is a member of the International Association of University Professors of English and the Kenan Ethics Advisory Council at Duke.

Professor Holloway has been the recipient of three Outstanding Book Awards from Choice Magazine, and has received the Anna Julia Cooper Scholar Award from St. Augustine's College; the Samuel DuBois Cook Pioneer Award from Duke University; the Outstanding Research Award and the Provost's Professional Development Award from North Carolina State and has been a recipient of the Rockefeller Foundation Fellowship. She is a member of The Links, Incorporated, and was received into the sisterhood of Chi Chapter of Alpha Kappa Alpha Sorority, Inc.—the same Talladega College undergraduate chapter as her mother Ouida.

In 1972, at Lincoln Memorial United Methodist Church in Buffalo, she married Russell Holloway—who holds an undergraduate degree from Talladega College and a graduate degree from Duke University where he is Associate Dean for Corporate and Industry Relations for Duke's Pratt School of Engineering. The Holloways are members of Davie Street Presbyterian Church in Raleigh, North Carolina. They are the parents of son Bem K., deceased, and daughter Ayana.

Samadah Nur

Samadah Nur, is the founder and Chief Executive Officer of An-Nur Creations, a family owned business based in Atlanta, GA. She was born in 1950 in Erie, PA to Khadijah Nur (Willie Mae Clanton Johnson) and Raymond Johnson. She was raised in Buffalo, New York along with her 13 brothers and sisters, including siblings from her father's second marriage. She has three sons, and is the proud grandmother of six.

Samadah belongs to the Abeynue Allahe Universal Arabic Association, Incorporated (AAUAAI) in Buffalo with headquarters in Arabia. She received an Associate's Degree in Early Childhood Education at Erie Community College in Buffalo. She was elected President of the Early Childhood Club at Erie County Community College and was awarded the Outstanding Teacher's award by the Early Childhood Education Department. She received her Bachelor's Degree in Social Science at San Jose State University in California.

Samadah started the school, "AN-NUR Day Care," and conduced the Islamic Children workshops at the Parker Street Masjid in Buffalo, New York. During the late 70's she established a Saturday school program, The Young Afrikan Sister Club, for girls between the ages of 5-13. Samadah also co-founded another Saturday school, called the Afrikan Studies Workshop, for both boys and girls ages five and older. She also taught at the Sunnyvale Montessori School in California and at the St. Augustine Child Development Center in Buffalo, New York where she received the Teacher of the Year Award.

She is the author of three books, *The Seven Powerful Words, All About Ramadan* and *My Calendar Book*. While working on her books, she was certified in sign language by the Martin Luther King Library Sign Language Department in Washington, DC. She has also published articles in the *Allstate Kids Quarterly* magazine and the "Kid's Korner" in *Al-Elaan*, an on-line newsletter. Samadah has also released two CDs; *Kwanzaa Time* and *Calling All Women.*

Samadah is a member of a number of organizations, including the National Black Herstory Task Force, headquartered in Atlanta, Metro

Atlanta Kwanzaa Association, Buffalo Kwanzaa Committee, Sisters United in Human Services, Inc., the African American Female Business Owners of the Atlanta Business League, and numerous others. She is also the chairperson of the Global Outreach committee of the National Black Herstory Task Force.

Samadah has received several public awards and honors including: The Apple Pie Award; Atlanta Artists Against Gun Violence; Million MOM March Chapter, Atlanta, Georgia; and Certificate of Continuing Education from the Department of Human Resources in Atlanta. The Calling All Women CD made history at the Fourth Annual National Black Herstory Conference and Awards Ceremony in March of 2001.

Connie Porter

Connie Rose Porter grew up in Lackawanna, New York, the second youngest of nine brothers and sisters. She was raised in a housing project in the city. She attended both the Lackawanna and Buffalo Public Schools, graduating from City Honors High School. She completed an undergraduate degree at the State University of New York at Albany in 1981. Ms. Porter earned an M.F.A. from Louisiana State University.

She was a fellow at Bread Loaf and was named a regional winner in Granta's Best Young American Novelist contest. She has taught English and creative writing at Milton Academy and Emerson College in Massachusetts and at Southern Illinois University at Carbondale.

Ms. Porter is the author of two novels *All Bright Court* and *Imani All Mine.* Her adult novel, *All-Bright Court,* was selected by the American Library Association as one of the Best Books of 1991. In addition, she authored the *Addy* books in the Pleasant Company's American Girls series. The *Addy* series has sold more than 3 million copies and were voted Best Children's Series of 1993 in the annual *Publishers Weekly* Cuffie Awards.

As a writer, she offers a strong voice for the characters in her books; the stories deal with being black, female, poor, marginalized and brilliant in demonstrating an ability to cope and find beauty within themselves and the world around them. Her book awards are numerous including the 1994 International Reading Association Children's Choice Award and the 1994 Children's Book Council Children's Choice Award.

Ms. Porter lives in Pittsburgh with her mother and 18-month old daughter.

Uncrowned Queens in Business

Wendy Anderson

Born in Alton, Illinois the third child of Melvin and Lena Harris, Wendy Christine Harris moved to Buffalo, New York with her family 9 months after she was born and considers herself a native Buffalonian. She is a graduate of Buffalo State College and is currently the owner of a home-based business. The business is called WORDS and Wendy serves nonprofit organizations and individuals in the areas of proposal/grant writing and program development.

She currently serves on the Board of Directors of the Precious Jewels Day Care Center and has served on other boards in the past. She is also active in her church, New Hope Baptist, where she serves as a Deaconess alongside her husband, Deacon James E. Anderson. She sings in the Gospel Choir, teaches Sunday School to adolescent children, and is a member of the Nurses Guild and the Women's United Choir.

Wendy is also an author. Her book, *The Art of Grantwriting* is a how-to guide for writing proposals. Wendy is presently working on a novel. She also writes feature articles for *The Word,* a local Christian newspaper.

Wendy feels very blessed to have a loving husband, a daughter and two sons. Amahl, the oldest son, lives in Las Vegas where he is studying for his bachelors' degree in Media Production at the University of Nevada. Anwar, the youngest son, received a fellowship from the University of Michigan at Ann Arbor where he is in a doctoral program and studying to be a pharmacologist/scientist. Safiya, her youngest child, is married with two sons, and living in Germany. She also has 2 grandsons, two living mothers, and a large extended family including seven brothers and sisters, nieces, nephews, and aunts, cousins, and others. To God be the Glory.

Mary Fisher

Mary N. Fisher was the first African American female realtor in Upstate New York. She founded the Mary N. Fisher Realty Company. With her knowledge of real estate issues, she became a consultant to the US Department of Housing and Urban Development (HUD) and was instrumental in helping to implement the federal government's 221 Program. Many prominent African American residents were her clients and she sold George K. Arthur and Thomas Edwards their first homes in Buffalo, New York.

Mrs. Fisher loved her community, demonstrating her commitment by raising funds for the Humboldt YMCA. As chairperson for their annual fundraising campaign she served with distinction from 1962-1967. Also, she held active membership in the National Association of Negro Business and Professional Women's Clubs.

An involved member of the Masonic Family, she held leadership positions denoting the highest level of service within two of these organizations. The first was Worthy Matron of Ionic Chapter # 77, Order of the Eastern Star, Prince Hall Affiliate. She was also the Illustrious Commandress of Hadja, Court #62, Daughters of Isis. She was an active member of Housing Opportunities Made Equal (HOME) , the NAACP and the Winsomettes.

She graduated from Hutchinson Central High School and Bryant and Stratton Business Institute. Mrs. Fisher also received specialized training from the National Association of Housing Specialists and The Home Owners Association.

She was married to Charley H. Fisher Jr. and is the mother of the Honorable Charley H. Fisher III.

Yvonne Hudson

Buffalo's own Yvonne Hudson has been an icon in the beauty industry for over 30 years. As the owner of Yvonne's Beauty Cutique, she credits success to her faith in God and the support of her husband.

Yvonne began her career in cosmetology working from the ground up. She began by working as a maid in the beauty shop in the old Hengerer's Department Store (which later became Kaufmann's) in Buffalo. She became more involved in the industry and pursued training at the Roberts School of Beauty. Her perseverance was realized as she became the first Black hair stylist at Hengerer's. Yvonne continued to hone her skills by attending advanced training at Dudley University.

After praying and asking the Lord for guidance and encouraged by her husband, Robert Hudson, and son, Keith Pollard, Yvonne opened Yvonne's Beauty Cutique in 1972. Thirty years later, she gives thanks for her blessings and begins and ends each day with prayer. As she puts it, "It makes good business sense to put God first, family second, and career third." Yvonne, true to her Virgo nature is a perfectionist, taking great pride in her work and putting forth every effort to ensure that her client's needs are met. A true testament to her skills and caring is evidenced in the fact that she has maintained clients from her Hengerer days. It has been a tradition in her salon to maintain a solid team of professionals. The salon has been recognized as a winner in many hair styling competitions as well as having been honored as the most professional salon in the area. Other stylists have been inspired to follow in her footsteps and like a Mother, she has nurtured, supported and encouraged her stylists to move on, while embracing and mentoring younger ones. On any given holiday, you will find former stylists returning to say hello. When asked why she has been so successful over the years, her answer is simple, "Every morning when I turn the key, I invite God in."

There's a time in everyone's life when one wishes to take it a bit easy and Yvonne plans to do just that by turning over the reins of *Yvonne's Beauty Cutique* to Lisa Daniels and Noel Mobley. She is not retiring, just taking a breather from the task of operating a business for over thirty years.

Yvonne and her husband, Robert, are very active members of Pleasant Grove Baptist Church. This leisure pace will afford them more time to visit family and friends, especially her grandson, Ian Sloane, of whom she's very proud.

Ada Talbert Jordan

Ada Talbert was born in 1854, the first child of Robert Talbert and Anna Harris Talbert. Her parents were considered one of the wealthiest black families at that time. She went to Catholic schools and was considered a formally educated lady for the times. She was the sister-in-law of Mary Burnett Talbert, who married her brother in 1891. She married John Jordan and from that union produced three daughters. For the majority of her life, however, she functioned as a single parent.

Education was highly prized by Ada Talbert Jordan. One of her daughters, Edith Jordan Rawlings, was one of the first blacks to graduate from Buffalo State Teachers College. Her family was extremely important to her throughout her life. She traveled extensively by train and enjoyed going to the spas in Saratoga to partake in the hot springs. Saratoga was noted for treatments that gave relief to an arthritic condition that she developed during her later years.

Mrs. Jordan had an eye for business. She survived during this time by managing and living off her share of her parent's estate, which consisted of income properties and other land holdings. She was one of very few individuals who built and maintained her own home before 1900 in Buffalo, New York. This was a remarkable deed in itself when so many people lost everything during the great depression of 1929. She exemplified the strength and resilience of black women, and set the standard for her children who passed on the same kind of fortitude to their children.

Ada Talbert Jordan died in 1938 and is buried in a family plot in Forest Lawn Cemetery.

Katherine Kirkland

Katherine Alexander Kirkland was born on March 2, 1919. She was the oldest of seven children (Alfred, George, Frank, Cora Lee Whitaker, Hattie Burroughs, and Elizabeth Alexander) born to the late Walter and Marie (nee Belton) Alexander of Camden, South Carolina. She accepted Christ at an early age and joined Zion Hill A.M.E. Church in Camden where she also attended school.

In 1942, she relocated to Buffalo, New York, and became a member of Pilgrim Baptist Church. She served on the church's usher board for 50 years and was honored as Usher of the Year by the Great Lakes Usher's Association. Her other awards include the Outstanding Service Award from the Health Unit of the Usher's Association, and the Moot Senior Citizens Center award for dedicated service. She was an avid member of Paramount Chapter #57, Order of the Eastern Star, Prince Hall Affiliate; The Floral Club; and the General Mission.

Known for her culinary skills, especially baking, she and her husband, Thomas, owned and operated a popular soul food restaurant, *Kirkland's Turquoise Diner.* Located at 1216 Jefferson Avenue, the restaurant remained in business from the 1960s until the early 1980s. In 1974, she was cited in *The Buffalo News* by columnist Ceaser Williams. *Kirkland's Diner* was the last restaurant she owned before retiring from the business. Later, the joy of cooking led her to accept part-time employment for several years at the Blessed Sacrament Catholic Church, from which she retired permanently. She also catered many affairs in the Buffalo area, and will always be remembered by family and friends for her annual Christmas Eve dinners.

Mrs. Kirkland and her husband had three children: son Alonzo of Brooklyn, New York, and son Theodore and daughter Jewell LaVern both of Buffalo. She was the proud grandmother of thirteen grandchildren and six great-grandchildren.

She died on June 24, 2002, at the age of 83 and is interred in Forest Lawn Cemetery.

Mary Alice Newkirk

Mary Alice Newkirk is a native of Deland, Florida. As a youth, she grew up in Cheyenne, Wyoming where she attended Cheyenne High School and played in the band until her senior year was completed. Music was her first love.

After high school, she attended Paul Quinn College, Waco Texas and graduated with a nursing degree in 1954. She received her license in the state of Texas and later became licensed in the states of New York and Florida. She moved to Buffalo, New York in 1960 and worked as a nurse at both Sisters Hospital and Buffalo General Hospital. She was also a private duty nurse for many years.

In 1991, she became the spokesperson for a newly formed interdenominational church, United Church of Faith, Inc. She was instrumental in helping the church secure 4.5 million dollars for the building and property. She later became the treasurer of the church and maintained a position on the Board of Directors and Board of Trustees.

Mary Alice is also an entrepreneur, owing and operating several businesses in Buffalo, including a music recording studio on Grand Island, New York. Newkirk Productions operated successfully for 12 years and was sold to Young Entertainment Systems in 1998.

Mary Alice is a member of the National Female Executive Club, and the Mary B. Talbert Civic and Cultural Club where she has served as Correspondence Secretary. She has served as Regional Board Chairperson and Current Membership Chairperson for the Empire State Federation of Women's Clubs, Inc. for the past ten years. She also served as Regional President - Buffalo/Rochester areas Northeastern Regional Organizer, National Association of Colored Women's Club Budget Committee, the Corporate Liaison Committee for Scholarships, and served with the Buffalo/Rochester 500 Club to recruit members.

Mary Alice Newkirk is heralded by many of her colleagues as an "unsung hero" because of her benevolence towards others and her willingness to work.

Virginia M. Price

Virginia M. Price was a leader who was recognized for her lifetime of service to her community. She was born Virginia Allen in Fairmont, West Virginia, but raised in Youngstown, Ohio. She graduated from Youngstown's Rayen High School in 1922 and moved to Buffalo that same year. She owned and operated her own business, the Style Beauty Salon, on Glenwood Avenue at Michigan Avenue for a number of years.

In 1932, she married Alfred D. Price, an Erie County employee who later became a public housing manager. A downtown housing project is now named for Mr. Price.

During World War II, Mrs. Price signed up for the Women's Army Corps, despite the fact that she was married and had a home of her own in Buffalo. She served as a sergeant at Fort Des Moines in Iowa, running cooking operations at the fort. "She was ahead of her time in many ways," recalled her son, Alfred. "Although we have no way of documenting or proving it, she may have been the first African American woman in Buffalo to own and operate her own automobile."

Mrs. Price assumed a leadership role in the Buffalo community when her son was attending School 53. She was elected president of the Parent-Teacher Association and built the school's PTA into the most active and engaged in the city – it had a 98 percent participation rate among parents. She also served three terms on the Niagara Frontier Association of PTA organizations.

She served for 33 years as a member of the Buffalo Chapter of The Links, Incorporated, a national organization of African American women. A charter member of the Buffalo chapter, Mrs. Price held a number of positions, including president, secretary, treasurer, and publicity chairwoman for the Ebony Fashion Fair, an annual scholarship benefit. During her tenure, the local group awarded about 125 scholarships to young women. Her son was awarded a National Achievement Scholarship, and she and her husband were proud that he became one of the first group of black graduates of Princeton University.

Mrs. Price represented The Links, Incorporated as an active member of the Buffalo Federation of Women's Clubs for 16 years and was chairwoman of the education committee of the federation for 12 years.

She served on the Board of Governors of the National Conference for Community and Justice for 21 years, until 1991. In 1974, she received the National Conference for Community and Justice (NCCJ) Brotherhood-Sisterhood Award for her community service. In 1996, she was again presented an award by the NCCJ for her lifetime contributions.

A lifelong Episcopalian, Mrs. Price was active in Church of the Ascension in Buffalo. She served as a member of the Altar Guild at Ascension for more than 30 years and was also twice elected to serve on the Vestry, the church's governing body. Until her retirement from active serve at the age of 90, Mrs. Price hand-embroidered all the fair linens used on the altar of the church.

Mrs. Price's long and productive life ended on March 30, 2003 at the age of 97. She was the proud mother of one son, Alfred; one grandson; three step-grandchildren; and four great-grandchildren. She is interred at Forest Lawn Cemetery.

Sundra Ryce

Ms. Ryce grew up in a family construction business and views the construction industry as a great business opportunity for women. She was born in Buffalo, New York and received her Bachelor of Science Degree in Business Studies from the University at Buffalo. After graduation, she worked as a manager in her father's company, WC Roberson Plumbing and Construction Corp. After a short time, she was encouraged by her father to start her own company.

She is currently the President and CEO of SLR Contracting Service Company, Inc., a general construction company headquartered in Buffalo, New York. The company was established in 1996 to provide quality work and exemplary customer service in the construction industry. The company's motto is "Building in Excellence, Constructing in Perfection."

Under her leadership, SLR has developed into an innovative and competitive construction company. SLR is a member of the Ciminelli Construction team in Buffalo, New York that will help oversee the $1 billion, 10-year Buffalo Public Schools renovation project.

Ms. Ryce and SLR have received numerous awards and recognition including the following: 2003, YWCA Leadership Award - Entrepreneur of the Year; 2003, SLR ranked No. 4 of the top 100 Fastest Growing Inner City Companies in America by ICIC and *Inc. Magazine;* 2002, Minority Small Business Person of the Year - U. S. Small Business Administration – Buffalo District; SLR named as one of Western New York's Top Private Companies for 2002 (*Business First*); 2002, SLR named as one of Buffalo - Niagara's Fastest Growing Companies; Fast Track 50 Award (*Business First*); 2002, Leadership Award - Erie County Executive, Joel Giambra; 2001, SLR ranked #10 in the Top 21 Women - Owned Businesses listed in *Business Women First* and many more. Her future plans for the company include an expansion in the Northeast and Southern regions of the United States.

Ms. Ryce is married to Stephen Ryce, SLR's Vice President, and is the mother of two children.

Thomasina Stenhouse

Dr. Stenhouse, more commonly known as "Tina," was born and raised in Buffalo, New York. She attended Howard University where she earned both a Bachelor of Arts degree in Sociology and a Master of Education degree in Student Personnel Administration.

Prior to completing the requirements for her M.Ed. degree, in 1973, Tina became a Recruitment Specialist at the Board of Governors of the Federal Reserve System. In 1981, a strong entrepreneurial desire led Tina to leave the Internal Revenue Service, Los Angeles District office, and begin a direct sales business. From 1985 to 1991, Tina added the private sector to her bank of human resources practitioner experiences, working for a large regional bank, and a highly diversified, multi-national, privately held holding company.

In 1991, Tina returned to school on a full-time basis to pursue a Ph.D. degree in Management, at the University at Buffalo. While a student, she worked as a university instructor, and as a human resources and organizational behavior consultant for several Western New York companies. Upon completion of her Ph.D. program requirements, Tina was hired as a Human Resources Manager and Corporate Trainer at Moog Incorporated.

As a member of Delta Sigma Theta Sorority, Inc., a public service sorority, for the past 33 years, Tina has held many elected offices. She twice chaired the local chapter's largest college scholarship fundraiser and most recently served as Vice President of the Buffalo Alumnae Chapter for the 1999-2001 biennium. In addition to her community work through Delta, Tina has held several ministerial leadership roles at New Life Assembly of God where she has been an active member for 20 years. In Spring 2003, under the covering of her home church, Tina began a new ministry for women through a bi-weekly, home-based, small group Bible study. She presently serves on one local board of governance, two advisory boards, and is the recipient of numerous academic honors and awards.

Her experiences and accomplishments confirm Psalm 32:8: *I will instruct you and teach you in the way you should go; I will counsel you and watch over you.* Tina currently resides in Buffalo, New York.

Mary Vance-Boyd

Mary Vance-Boyd, is a native of Mason, Tennessee. Mary began her long association with Manufacturers and Traders Trust Company (M&T Bank) in 1977. She rose thru the ranks from Teller to Head Teller, Administrative Coordinator, and Personal Bank Advisor before becoming an Assistant Bank Manager in 1986. In 1990, she earned a Bachelor of Science in Management. Recognizing her extraordinary skills in working with people, M&T promoted her to Branch Manager for Jefferson Marketplace where she served from 1988-1994. Mary was successful in advancement in the management ranks at M&T, and became Branch Manager for the new Towne Gardens Plaza Branch, a position she held from 1994 until her retirement in March, 2002. She is the only African American in Buffalo to start and develop two bank branches. For example, under her management, the Jefferson Marketplace branch grew from zero to 8 million, and she repeated a similar success at the Towne Gardens branch.

While at M&T, Mary engaged in a number of important community activities including a school banking program in 1991 and initiated the annual Towne Garden Appreciation Day in 1995. In 1989 she was also instrumental in implementing the framework for the Greater Eastside Business Association.

Some of her many community affiliations include board member of the following: Greater Eastside Business Association [secretary]; G.R.O.U.P. Ministries; William-Emslie YMCA; Urban Banker, Buffalo Chapter; Public School #53 and Futures Academy. Mary is also a member of the NAACP; the National Rainbow Coalition, Inc.; Financial Women International and GospelFest.

She has received numerous awards including: the Small Business Administration, Black Achievers Award, the Southern Christian

Leadership Conference Community Service, Certificate of Merit from Erie County Legislator for the Third District and the Martin Luther King, Jr. Business Award Certificate of Achievement for dedicated service within the Buffalo Community

She is the mother of four daughters, Natalie, Kim, Debbie, all of Buffalo, and Cacine who resides in Baltimore. She also has six grandchildren. Mary lives with her husband Robert in Grand Island, and believes that she is an instrument used to glorify God. Mary is a member of St. John Baptist Church and serves on numerous committees and task forces.

Mary-Frances Winters

Mary-Frances Winters is president and founder of The Winters Group, Inc., a Rochester-based consulting firm with a national client roster. The Winters Group specializes in research, strategic planning, training and public speaking with emphasis in ethnic and multicultural issues.

Prior to founding The Winters Group in 1984, Ms. Winters was affirmative action officer and senior market analyst at Eastman Kodak Company, where she worked for eleven years.

The Niagara Falls, New York native is a graduate of the University of Rochester with undergraduate degrees in English and Psychology, and a Master's degree in business administration from the William E. Simon Executive Development Program. She received an honorary doctorate from Roberts Wesleyan College in 1997.

Ms. Winters was selected to serve as Rochester Institute of Technology's College of Continuing Education's 1994-95 Distinguished Minett Professor where she taught a leadership course entitled, "21st Century Leader: Visionary, Inspired, and Spiritually Grounded," at the graduate level.

Ms. Winters has received numerous awards and honors including the "Minority Business Person of the Year" received from the Rochester Minority Enterprise Development Committee in 1988. She was featured in the 1989 edition of Marquis *Who's Who in American*

Women, and was the 1991 recipient of the Athena Award by the Women's Council of the Greater Rochester Metro Chamber of Commerce. In 1992 she was one of five women nationally to receive the Avon Products, Inc., and U.S. Small Business Administration's Women of Enterprise Award. In 1994 she received the Urban League's Outstanding Community Leader Award. Ms. Winters was selected as one of Rochester's torch bearers for the 1996 Olympic Torch Relay. Phi Delta Kappa Education Fraternity presented Ms. Winters with its 1996 Research Award.

The Winters Group clients include corporate, government, education, and not-for-profits such as Eastman Kodak, Xerox Corporation, AT&T, IBM, E.I. DuPont de Nemours and Co., Chase Manhattan Bank, N.A., Lawyers Cooperative Publishing Company, Council on Foundations, United Way, National Center on Education and Economy, Rochester City School District, City of Rochester, and Rochester Institute of Technology.

A member of the Board of Trustees of the University of Rochester, Ms. Winters also serves on the board of the Greater Rochester Metro Chamber of Commerce, Chase Manhattan Bank of Rochester, and Roberts Wesleyan College. She has previously served on the boards of Rochester Area Foundation; United Way; McQuaid Jesuit High School; Blue Cross/Blue Shield of the Rochester Area; McCurdy and Co., Inc.; and the National Board of Directors for Girl Scouts of the USA; among others. She also is a member of the National Speakers Association.

She is past chairperson of the Advisory Committee of the Greater Rochester Women's Fund, past president of the Girl Scouts of Genesee Valley, Inc., and the Black Business Association of Rochester. Ms. Winters was the 1994 General Campaign Chair for the United Way/Red Cross Campaign.

She is a frequent contributor to the editorial page of the local newspaper on topics of education and diversity. She has been published in the *International Personnel Management Association Newsletter* and has written monographs on "Philanthropy Among People of Color" for the Council on Foundations in Washington, DC.

Ms. Winters, a widow, has two children, Mareisha and Joe. She resides in Fairport, New York and is a member of Alpha Kappa Alpha Sorority, Inc. and The Links, Incorporated. She is an active member of Mt. Olivet Baptist Church.

Uncrowned Queens in Community and Social Service Organizations

Janet E. Barnes

Janet E. Barnes is an experienced public school administrator, teacher of music, and community activist. She earned a B.A., Ed.M., Specialist in Education Administration, and MS in Public Affairs from the University at Buffalo. Since 1995 she has served as an Assistant Principal at Buffalo Traditional School in Buffalo, New York. Her professional experience before this position included serving as Coordinator, Buffalo Alternative School; Teacher, Buffalo Schools; Administrative Intern, Kensington Preparatory and BVTC and Teacher/Administrative Assistant in Buffalo Public Schools. She has educated thousands of students academically and emotionally; building self-esteem and lifting goals in those with exceptional needs. Among her teaching and administrative career highlights she includes assisting with planning and implementing the EPIC Program parent, student and teacher workshops. In conjunction with Raymond Perreault, she also reorganized and improved the Buffalo Alternative Junior High School seventh and eighth grade satellites.

A devoted musician, Janet has worked for over twelve years as the Church musician for First Trinity Lutheran Church in Buffalo. Prior to this she was Organist and Choir Director for Calvary CME Church also in Buffalo. She was a guest vocalist at the Alpha Kappa Alpha Sorority, Inc. National Convention in Indianapolis, Indiana. In addition, she played keyboard and sang on Quest, a nationally released cassette recording.

Janet works to encourage other individuals' participation in the performing arts. She coordinated a Buffalo-based Talent Competition for Omega Psi Phi Fraternity and served as a judge during the Fraternity's National Talent Program in Baltimore, Maryland. Locally, she organized and directed a talent showcase that was presented by Buffalo Public School students in the Marquee for three consecutive years.

Her professional affiliations and elected positions include President, National Association of Negro Business and Professional Women's Clubs; Treasurer, St. Andrews Board of Managers; Buffalo

Council of School Administrators; Immediate Past President, Alpha Kappa Alpha Sorority, Inc., Gamma Phi Omega Chapter; Trustee, Elite Temple #143; Northeast District Corresponding Secretary, National Association of Negro Business and Professional Women's Clubs; Honorary member and Awards Committee member, Alpha Kappa Alpha Sorority, Inc.; and member of the Erie County Chapter of The Links, Incorporated.

In addition to the above-referenced affiliations, she has several community affiliations. These include past Secretary, Metropolitan Democratic Club; Buffalo Political Women's Network; present Educational Advisor and past Secretary, North Fillmore Democratic Club; Advisory Council Member, Artists of African Descent; past Committee-Woman and Secretary, Fourth Zone Democratic Organization; present Senior Vice President, Housing Opportunities Made Equal and the Colored Musicians Club. Awards and achievements include the True Bethel Church Task Force, Community Service Award; Alpha Kappa Alpha Sorority, Inc., Gamma Phi Omega Chapter, Outstanding Music Award; Alpha Kappa Alpha Sorority, Inc., Gamma Phi Omega Chapter, Leadership Award; Canisius College, Partner in Education Award; Fourth Zone Democratic Club, Outstanding Educator Award; First Trinity Church, Divine Servant Award; Alpha Kappa Alpha Sorority, Inc., Outstanding Talent Competition Award and numerous others.

Thelma C. Batts

Mrs. Thelma Clarice Batts was born to Hilgrove and Geraldine Adderley in Pembroke, West Bermuda on July 16, 1924. Throughout her lifetime she has lived in various foreign countries with her spouse, e.g. Japan, England, Bermuda and concluded her military travel when Sgt. Batts was assigned to Niagara Falls Air Force Base.

After the loss of her husband while he was on a tour of duty in Korea, Mrs. Batts established residence in Buffalo, New York with her only daughter, Patricia Clark, who is also an Uncrowned Queen. While in Buffalo, she began her volunteer service with the breakfast and lunch programs at Public School 23. Through her diligence and love for the community and children, she enrolled in Bennett High School and received her diploma with awards and honors. Mrs. Batts then began employment as a Teacher's Aide. For years she worked with Pre-Kindergarten students at both schools 23 and 17. She was also an active member of the Parent Teachers Association. She is an active member of the William Emslie YMCA and St. Philip's Episcopal Church where she serves on the Committee for Episcopal Church Women's Organization, Chaplain; the Altar Guild; and St. Philip's Annual Festival.

Mrs. Batts was formerly a member of the board of directors for the Niagara Frontier Association for Sickle Cell Disease, Inc., where in 1986 she received an award for fundraising efforts; Geneva B. Scruggs Community Health Care Center; the Women for Human Rights and Dignity program; the St. Augustine's Center Board of Directors and the Amsterdam Street Block Club. She has received awards from the YMCA Partners for Youth for service, Salvation Army Golden Age Center for Cooperation and Sportsmanlike Conduct during the 2000 Olympics and numerous others.

Thelma has received numerous certificates of appreciation including the YMCA Century Club for "generous support of YMCA programs" and a Proclamation from Women for Human Rights and Dignity for "giving countless hours of volunteer service over and above the call of duty."

At age 70, the Common Council City of Buffalo proclaimed "July 16, 1993 - Thelma C. Batts Day in the City of Buffalo." Thelma has also received proclamations of appreciation for her service from Governor Mario Cuomo and Congressman Jack Quinn.

Mrs. Thelma Batts retired from the Board of Education in 1992 and continues to serve the Buffalo community as a dedicated volunteer in various progressive organizations. Mrs. Batts has three grand children, DeAnna and Jaye who reside in Baltimore, Maryland and Devon who resides in Seattle, Washington.

Jessie Faye Ector

Jessie Faye Ector was born in Buffalo to Grover, Sr. and Ethel Coleman. She is a graduate of Fosdick Masten High School and Medaille College where she received a B.S. Degree in Business Administration.

She joined the Mary B. Talbert Civic and Cultural Club in 1993 and had the distinction of being Club President from 1998 through 2001. She served in the office of Recording Secretary at the local, regional, and state levels and is Financial Secretary for both the local club and the Buffalo Region.

Other volunteer community activities include Junior Achievement, Boy Scouts of America, the Diabetes Association and Heart Association. Jessie has been employed at the Tonawanda Engine Plant, Powertrain Division of General Motors for the past 25 years. She has held positions in purchasing, quality control, and is currently a contract administrator with production control and logistics. Prior to joining General Motors, Jessie was employed with various community service organizations including Council on Culture Freedom School, Opportunities Development Corporation and the Contractor's Training Development Corporation.

Jessie is a life-long member of St. John Baptist Church where she serves faithfully with the Number 2 Usher Ministry and currently holds the position of Vice President. She is also a member of the Board of Christian Education Ministry.

She is the widow of William Ector, Sr. and the proud mother of William, Jr. of Atlanta, Georgia.

Yvonne Boyles Evans

Yvonne began her career with the Internal Revenue Service in 1974 as a Taxpayer Service Representative. After a series of promotions and increasing responsibility, she became the Employee/Community Liaison Officer for the Northeast Area of Internal Revenue Service. She is responsible for improving employee job satisfaction and increasing the visibility of IRS as an agency in the community that will ultimately positively impact voluntary compliance.

Yvonne has both initiated and supported numerous programs to provide developmental opportunities for young people with an emphasis on women and minorities, e.g., the Buffalo Urban League Job Training Program.

Yvonne is a silver and life member of Alpha Kappa Alpha Sorority, Inc., and is the immediate past President of the Gamma Phi Omega Chapter, serving in this capacity for four years. She also served as the Vice President for four years and was the Graduate Advisor to the Gamma Iota undergraduate chapter for thirteen years. As Graduate Advisor, she was responsible for monitoring the program activities of countless college students all of whom have achieved considerable successes in their careers.

Yvonne also coordinates many community outreach activities for the Internal Revenue Service including the Meals on Wheels, the United Way Day of Caring Project and many others. Her membership in clubs and other organizations is extensive and includes The Buffalo Chapter of The Links, Incorporated, the National Association of Negro Business and Professional Women's Clubs, the Buffalo Junior League, and the American Association of University Women.

Numerous agencies benefit from her board memberships including the Buffalo and Erie County Historical Society Board of Managers, the Buffalo Alliance for Education and the YWCA of Western New York, Nominating Committee. Yvonne also completed the prestigious "Leadership Buffalo" training in 2002 and she is a member of the Community Facilitation Team for the organization.

The community has recognized Yvonne with countless awards and citations for her professional and community work including the Black Achievers in Industry Award, Federal Woman of the Year Award, YWCA Outstanding Leadership Achievement Award, Department of the Treasury Distinguished Performance Award, Alpha Kappa Alpha Sorority, Inc., Outstanding President Award and National Conference for Community and Justice Brotherhood and Sisterhood Award for Community Service/Volunteerism.

Yvonne is a member of St. John Baptist Church where she serves on the Board of Education Ministry.

She is the proud daughter of Leona and the late Otto Boyles, who inspired her to become the person she is today. She is married to Kermit Allen Evans. They have two sons Karlton and Keith and three grandchildren Marriza, Justin and Amara. Yvonne believes that "Through God all things are possible."

Martha Antoinette Ford

At the turn of the twentieth century Martha Ford was among the black club women in Buffalo who advocated for the rights of blacks. She was married to Cornelius Ford, a successful businessman who moved to Buffalo in 1906. Mr. Ford was a prominent livestock dealer who was the only black member of the Buffalo Livestock Association. Armour and Company, the world's largest meat packing company at the time, was one of Ford's customers.

Mrs. Ford was active in the Buffalo Chapter of the National Association for the Advancement of Colored People (NAACP) and was the first president of that organization's Women's Auxiliary. That group established three committees: Education, Fundraising, and Entertainment. These committees organized cultural events, baby contests, beauty pageants and other projects to raise funds and the visibility of the NAACP in the city. Mrs. Ford was also a founder of the Douglass Club of Colored Women as well as The Dames. The Dames was organized to provide its members with activities centered on cards and social/cultural activities.

Mrs. Ford died on January 24, 1936, and is buried at Forest Lawn Cemetery.

Jeanne Gaye

Jeanne Gaye was born in Washington, D.C. and graduated from Cardozo High School. She attended American University, Temple Business School and later Watterson College in Louisiana. She married her high school sweetheart and had five children. Jeanne worked in the federal government for 15 years. She moved to Los Angeles, California in 1971.

In 1988 she became an ordained minister and in 1991 became a member of the United Church of Faith, Inc. She later became a member of its Board of Directors and served in that capacity for four years. She has a special interest in children and is an author of children's books and has been a member of the Buffalo Literary Guild for five years.

Her civic and volunteer activities include: Chairperson of the Board of Directors for the United Church of Faith, Inc.; Vice President and past Recording Secretary of the Mary B. Talbert Civic and Cultural Club; Member of the National Association of Colored Women's Clubs, Inc.; past Recording Secretary of the Empire State Federation of Women's Clubs, Inc.; a 25 year member of the Eastern Stars and past Assistant Secretary of the Northeastern Federation of Women's and Youth Clubs, Inc.

Jeanne is the sister of the late Marvin P. Gaye, Jr. and served as past Chairperson of the Board of Directors to the Marvin P. Gaye Memorial Foundation. Her latest endeavor is establishing I Am the Children, Inc. a foundation dedicated to children.

Marietta Dabney Gayle

Marietta Dabney Gayle joined the Mary B. Talbert Civic and Cultural Club in 2000. She was a delegate to the 2001 Empire State Federation Convention, where she won the hearts of her club sisters. Marietta is Sunshine Chairperson of the Mary B. Talbert Civic and Cultural Club and Corresponding Secretary of the Buffalo Region of the Empire State Federation of Women's Clubs, Inc.

The Mary B. Talbert Civic and Cultural Club considers it an honor that she has chosen to use her wealth of knowledge and experience in support of the club's service activities. She is an inspiration to all of the members with her poise, charm and tireless energy.

With a Master's Degree in Social Work from Columbia University School of Social Work, Marietta was employed in the Y.W.C.A. in Brooklyn, Newark, Bridgeport and Philadelphia, as well as Friendly Inn Settlement House in Cleveland, Ohio, prior to returning to Western New York. In Buffalo, she worked at the YWCA and the Children's Aid Society before retiring.

Even now, Marietta maintains her interest in continuing education and is considering going back to school to further her studies in the field of human relations. She would like to focus on children and adolescents and their families within the context of neighborhoods and communities. She would like to be able to help children, adolescents, their parents and/or grandparents create a more satisfying and meaningful existence in today's fast paced and challenging times. Her goal is to help families have fun in spite of the trials and tribulations they have experienced.

She is a member of Alpha Kappa Alpha Sorority, Inc., New York State Chapter of the National Association of Social Workers, St. Andrew's Episcopal Church and A.A.R.P. Marietta participates regularly, in the Senior Centers of the Salvation Army, the Emslie Street YMCA and the Senior Water Workout at the YWCA. She has also been appointed to the Board of Directors of Canaan House.

Marietta is the proud mother of five children. Her travels have taken her to South Africa, Senegal, the Dominican Republic, and Barbados as well as several states. She has also traveled to Switzerland to visit her son, a federal official, and his family.

Lula Lucritia Adams Gayles

Lula Lucritia Adams was born in Savannah, Georgia in 1918. Her parents, Maze Gregg Adams and Edna Earl Miller Adams moved to Buffalo when their daughter was just eight months old. Lula met and married Edward Cato Gayles, II in 1935. They were the proud parents of seventeen children.

She is remembered as an unselfish woman who put God, her husband and her children first. Her daughter and namesake, Lula Lucritia Gayles Herring, recalled that her mother waited for seven years to buy a dress in order to help her husband pay for the mortgage on their home at 325 South Division Street. Mrs. Gayles made homemade ice cream and crocheted doilies, handbags, hats, centerpieces, and dresses to help her husband, a 45-year employee of Bethlehem Steel Plant, provide for the family. As a result of her parents' efforts, Mrs. Herring said that the family always owned their own home and never knew the unfortunate problems large families sometimes face, such as being unable to pay household bills or needing charitable donations.

Mrs. Gayles was a strict disciplinarian who taught her children not to fight. Her children were not only obedient to her, but were respectful to all adults.

Throughout her life, Mrs. Gayles received numerous honors and recognition awards. The Governor, the Mayor, the Buffalo Common Council, social and church organizations honored Mrs. Gayles and her family (The Gayles Family Singers).

Her son, Gregg coined the phrase, "Love, Mamo," to express how her family feels about the outstanding contributions that Mrs. Gayles made to her family, the community of Buffalo, State of New York, the United States, and the world.

As a final expression of the legacy of this outstanding woman, the epithet on Mrs. Gayles' tombstone reads, "To live in the hearts of her seventeen children is not to die."

Ruby Lee Granberry

Ruby Lee Benton was born on April 29th to the late Reverend and Mrs. James Benton. The third of five children, she attended Public School #75 and graduated from Hutchinson Central High School. After an educational hiatus, during which she married Charles E. Grandberry, II, and raised two sons, Charles III (Tony) and Kevin (Veny); she returned to the world of academia. She graduated from Erie Community College in 1982. In addition, she took courses from the University of Buffalo, State Teachers College, and Trocaire College. She also taught "Human Growth and Development" to high school and junior high students and to young people at community youth centers as well as other special groups in Erie County and the surrounding area.

Although retired as a full time nurse, she has remained active by channeling her energy in a variety of positive ways. As a member of the Mary B. Talbert Civic and Cultural Club for over thirty years, she has served as Past President, Parliamentarian and chaired the Annual Awards Tea. This event recognizes 8th grade students on the threshold of high school who have demonstrated meritorious improvement in character and academics. Her volunteer work includes Meals on Wheels, Pastoral Care, Soup Kitchen and fundraising activities for Cancer Research. Ruby has also worked as a volunteer receptionist at Buffalo General Hospital and donated her time as a Counselor at Haven House, a crisis center for abused women and children.

Through all the years of being a dutiful wife, loving mother, tireless worker and faithful friend, one thing has remained constant; her faith in God. As a lifelong member of Mount Olive Baptist Church, founded by her father, her contributions, such as Choir Director and Usher Board member are too numerous to list. She continues to sing in two choirs and has enjoyed singing melodic lullabies to her two grandchildren, Marques and Raven.

G. Jean Howard

Born in Greensboro, North Carolina, Howard received her B.A. Degree from Bennett College, a M.S. in Education from Indiana University, Bloomington, Indiana, and completed course work certification Program Evaluation Systems at Cornell University. She has served as Executive Director of Wilson Commencement Park (WCP) since it opened in 1990 and was responsible for both the completion and oversight since inception of facilities' construction and program design. She was also responsible for management of a welfare reform and life skills organization which has provided services through several business units (Housing, Case Management, Mentoring, Employment, Literacy, Community Outreach, and Early Childhood Services) to over 750 single-parent families and children who seek increasing self-sufficiency and alternatives to welfare dependency. Under Jean's leadership, Wilson Commencement Park has grown from a small, community-based program to now serving as a model for community collaboration and a benchmark for welfare reform; both locally and nationally.

Prior to employment at Wilson Commencement Park, Jean served in senior management positions at the United Cerebral Palsy Association of Rochester; Clinic Coordinator for Substance Abuse/Maternal Infant Care Services at Hutzel Hospital, Detroit, Michigan; Project Manager, Well-Being Services for the Aging, Detroit, Michigan; Adult Program Director, Y.W.C.A., Springfield, Massachusetts; and the New York City Mission Society as a Case Manager.

Her community service is extensive. She served under Governor Mario Cuomo for six years on the Executive Committee of the New York State Office on Mental Retardation and Development Disabilities Advisory Council and was an advisor to the Governor's Office in the implementation of the Willowbrook Consent Decree. As an extension of her outreach, Jean served in an appointed position by Monroe County Executive, John Doyle, as Chair of the Day Care Consortium.

Jean's current community involvement includes: board of trustee membership at Bennett College, Monroe Community College, the Pluta Family Cancer Center Foundation, Energy East Corporation, Center for Governmental Research, the Women's Health Partnership, the Greater Rochester Metro Chamber of Commerce, the New York State Welfare Reform Block Grant Advisory Council, and the Rochester Chapter of The Links, Incorporated.

Her past trustee involvement over the past decade includes Genesee Hospital, Housing Council of Rochester, Otieana Council of the Boy Scouts of America, WXXI Broadcasting Council, State University of New York at Brockport's Educational Opportunity Center, Rochester School for the Deaf, Coordinated Care Services, Inc., Baden Street Settlement House, the Martin Luther King Commission, Mary Cariola Children's Center, and numerous other community service activities

Jean is a graduate of Leadership America, the country's only national not-for-profit leadership program for women of achievement. She is also the recipient of the Rochester Chapter of The Links, Incorporated White Rose award; the American Diabetes Association Woman of Valor award and the Athena Award Nominee. She received the Director's Award from the Greater Rochester Association of Women Attorneys and the March of Dimes Mother's of the Year award.

Jean is the mother of three adult children and a granddaughter.

Doris Jones

Doris W. Jones was described by those who knew and loved her as "...a strong voice, tenacious fighter and compassionate conscience for tenants and tenants rights in the Niagara Falls community, even in the face of strong adversity and opposition."

Doris was born in 1935 in Red Level Alabama. Her parents were Rufus and Rosie Jones. Doris moved to Niagara Falls, New York in 1944, where she began her advocacy to promote self-sufficiency and improve the overall quality of life for public housing residents. In 1975, Doris was elected President of the Center Court Tenant Association. In 1976, she was elected to the Niagara Falls Housing Authority Board of Commissioners, where she served for more than twenty-five years. She successfully initiated a variety of programs for the Niagara Falls Housing Authority including: The Summer Enrichment Program, Livin' Large and I Can Read Tutorial Programs, Annual Run from Drugs, Annual Thanksgiving Feast, and a host of job development and training programs. She developed numerous partnerships with local community agencies and organizations and was instrumental in obtaining funding for several of the Housing Authority's mentoring programs and activities.

In 2001, Doris received the distinguished Resident of the Year award from the National Association of African Americans in Housing at their annual conference in San Francisco. In 2002, she was the recipient of the Dr. Martin Luther King, Jr. Civil Rights Award. In her acceptance speech, she stated "I have tried to live my life similarly to the following quotation that I heard from Rev. Dr. Martin Luther King himself. *The ultimate measure of a man is not where he stands in movement of comfort and convenience, but where he stands in times of challenge and controversy.*"

Doris was a founding member of the Niagara Improvement Association and an instrumental member of the Niagara County Black Achievers, Inc. Her humanitarian efforts earned her certificates of meritorious service. She was inducted into the Housing Authority's "Wall of Fame" in 1992. In 1998, she received the "Heroes of Public

Housing" Award from the United States Department of Housing and Urban Development for her dedication and loyalty to the Housing Authority and its residents and for her constant encouragement. In 2002, she was honored at the Niagara Falls Housing Authority's 60th Anniversary Celebration with the distinguished "People and Possibilities" Award for service with distinction. Doris served as a 2nd Legislative District committeewoman for over forty-five years.

Miss Jones worked tirelessly as an Elections Inspector and held various positions with the Niagara County Department of Social Services and Mt. Saint Mary's Hospital. She was a faithful member of the New Jerusalem Revival Center Independent Church of God in Christ and always let her strong faith in God be her guide.

She had a strong love for children and often commented, "they are where our future lie, we all must be role models and nurture these children so that they can reach their full potential." In addition to her son, Raymond, she had three grandchildren whom she adored.

Doris W. Jones died on September 11, 2002. If Doris could be described succinctly, there would be just three words to describe this incredible woman, "Political and Community Activist, Advocate and Friend."

Wygenia (Genia) Hailstock Miles

Born in Newberry, South Carolina, Wygenia (Genia) Hailstock Miles moved to Buffalo in 1953 with her parents, the late Hattie Bell (Johnson) and Eugene Hailstock, five sisters and one brother. The family settled into the East side of Buffalo.

Mrs. Miles attended Buffalo Public Schools, The University at Buffalo, SUNY Empire State College, and Daemen College. She holds New York State Teacher Certification in Secondary Business Education, a Bachelor of Science Degree in Business Management with a Minor in Economics, and a Master of Business Administration with a concentration in International Studies. Genia has taught Business/Computers in the Buffalo Public School System since 1994. Other positions have included Deputy Director of the University at Buffalo/Bob Lanier

Center for Educational, Physical and Cultural Development, and Director of the University at Buffalo Institute for CBO Education and Training, and Administrative Associate with St. Augustine's Center, Inc.

Mrs. Miles is an educator whose goal is to help young people to grow toward becoming full participating members, prepared to become the leaders of our community. She believes that, "To whom much is given, much will be expected," Luke 12:48.

An active advocate for her community, Genia has held leadership positions in several professional and civic organizations, including Junior Achievement, Western New York School Advisory Board; Vice President, The Niagara Falls Chapter of The Links, Incorporated; Secretary, Fund Raising Chair and By-Laws Chair Harriet Tubman 300's; Leadership Buffalo Class of 1992; President of the Buffalo Alumnae Chapter of Delta Sigma Theta Sorority, Inc., an international public service organization; and Event Chairperson for the acclaimed St. Philip's Boys and Girls Choir.

Genia has also been an active member of St. Philip's Episcopal Church, where she served as Warden, Treasurer, and Chair of the Rector Search Committee; Vice-President of the St. Philip's Community Center, Secretary and Member of the Executive Committee Episcopal Community Services.

Genia Miles is married to William A. Miles, Sr. They are the parents of five children, Michelle Lynn (Robert) Sessum, William A. Miles, Jr., Simone Y. (Anthony) Harmon, (deceased), Michael L, Miles, and Jason E. Miles. She has 10 grandchildren and 1 great-grandchild.

Hortense Butts Nash

Hortense Butts Nash is the eldest of two daughters born to George and Ruby Tucker Butts. Hortense was born on September 29, 1925 in Atlanta, Georgia. Two years later, her sister Gloria was born in the family's new hometown of Ashville, North Carolina. In 1937, the Butts family relocated to Buffalo, New York.

Hortense attended the Buffalo Public Schools and continued her education at Buffalo State Teacher's College where she earned a Bachelor of Science in Elementary Education, in 1947. Ten years later, she was awarded a Master of Education degree in Educational Administration and Supervision from the University at Buffalo. Hortense also completed post-graduate studies in Corrective and Remedial Reading at Canisius College. In 1987, she received an OSHA Industrial Safety Certificate from Cornell University.

An accomplished musician, Hortense has pursued organ and liturgical studies with Helen Townsend Garretson, Squire Haskin, Dr. Roberta Bitgood, and Elaine Gardner. All of her instructors were church organists and former Deans of the American Guild of Organists.

Hortense began her teaching career in 1947 as a 6th grade teacher. She points out that her salary at that time was $2,900 a year. She was also a Corrective Reading Teacher at Martin Luther Christian School and in the Buffalo Public Schools system. She has mentored adults and children as a volunteer for Literacy, Inc. and also for an education project sponsored by the Erie County Chapter of The Links, Incorporated.

Hortense notes, "during my years of teaching, musicianship, and volunteerism, I have seen and responded to changes and innovations involving rules, techniques, and tastes. In these situations of transition, especially in the contexts of church music, I have been encouraged to help parents to encourage their children to learn the rudiments and basics so they will be able to perform and compete globally." Her life is guided by a scripture from Micah 6:8, "What does the Lord require, but to seek justice, be merciful, and walk humbly with God?"

In addition to teaching in the Buffalo Public Schools, Hortense has been an active volunteer in her community and church. Her affiliations include Life membership in the NAACP, the American Association of University Women, a 30-year member of the American Guild of Organists, and the National Association of Negro Business and Professional Women's Clubs, Inc. In the latter organization, she has served as Chapter President and Director of the national Choir, and is a life member. She is also a member of the New York State and the Buffalo Retired Teacher's Associations; a 50 year member of Delta Sigma Theta Sorority, Inc.; Erie County Chapter of The Links, Incorporated; Jack and Jill of America, Inc.; Pi Lambda Theta National Honor Society and the Friend's Book Club.

Hortense was the Treasurer of Women for Human Rights and Dignity, Inc. for thirteen years and volunteered with that group at Albion Correctional Facility, Erie County Holding Center and "Dignity Circle" Planning Committee. She is a former member of the historic Michigan Avenue Baptist Church and served as the Sunday School Superintendent and organist during the years she attended the church from 1942 to 1952. She is a member of St. Philip's Episcopal Church and has served as the organist and adult choir director. She has also held the offices of Junior and Senior Warden of the Church, Stewardship Committee Chair, Assistant Superintendent of the Sunday School, Sunday School Teacher, Acolyte Mother and Vestry Member.

Hortense has been honored by numerous organizations. She received the National Sojourner Truth Award from the National Association of Negro Business and Professional Women's Clubs in 1986 and the St. Philip's Episcopal Church Men's Club Service Award during the same year. The Buffalo Chapter of Jack and Jill of America, Inc. presented her the This Is Your Life Award and the Urban League recognized her as the Mother of the Year in 1980. She also received the 2002 Chairperson's Award from Women for Human Rights and Dignity, Inc.

Hortense and her husband, Jesse E. Nash, Jr. have jointly been recognized by the Buffalo NAACP, The Medgar Evers Award; AKA Sorority, Xi Epsilon Omega Chapter, The Black Family Award; The Buffalo Kwanzaa Committee, Community Service Award; Juneteenth,

Inc., Parade Marshals and the Buffalo Urban League, Family of the Year Award.

Hortense and Jesse have been married for over 50 years and have three children, Jesse III, George Raymond and Deborah Nash Franklin. Hortense keeps busy in her retirement by reading and collecting biographies and mysteries, travel, crossword puzzles and word games and of, course, music.

Sheila J. Nickson

Sheila J. Nickson is a native Buffalonian. Her family has lived in Buffalo since 1834. She attends St. Philip's Episcopal Church where over six generations of her family have been members since the founding of the church in the late 1800s. She has two sons, Stephen and Rodrick and two grandchildren, Alannah and Myles. Her early formal education began at P.S. #17 and Lafayette High where she was taught by many of the same teachers who taught her mother.

She went on to Buffalo State College when it was still the Buffalo Teachers College. Returning as an employee in the late sixties, Sheila joined the Chemistry Department professional staff. Her next position at Buffalo State College was Director of Affirmative Action . In the early 1970's Sheila served as statewide chair of the State University of New York (SUNY) Women's Caucus and recognized the need for an organization to respond to the needs of Black faculty and staff. She organized the SUNY Black Faculty and Staff Association statewide as well as the chapter at Buffalo State College.

Sheila was also involved in other SUNY-wide activities while on leave from Buffalo State College. She worked in Albany with Chancellor Boyer and Chancellor Wharton. At SUNY Central, Sheila continued advocacy activities for affirmative action programs and initiatives and was active in forming the national affirmative action organization. Moreover, she worked with Buffalo State's Educational Opportunity Program and International Education Officers and initiated a study tour to Senegal (West Africa). Sheila's ten years of tours and other efforts on behalf of Malika Village in West Africa led to their naming the Women's Social Center in the Malika Village after her. She continues to work on behalf of her adopted Malika Family.

Over the years, Sheila's community activities have paralleled her campus involvement including such activities as the BUILD Education Subcommittee, the Committee for Community Politics, founding member of the Northern Region Black Political Caucus and appointment by former Governor Mario Cuomo to the New York State Human Rights Advisory Council.

She also served on the National Urban League's Educational Advisory Council for five years and is past National President of the American Association for Affirmative Action. She was a founding member of the Afro-American Historical Association of the Niagara Frontier and served on the AA and R Committee of the United Way. She belongs to the National Women's Political Caucus, National Organization of Women (NOW), the Executive Board of the SUNY Black Faculty Association, Western New York Council for African Relief, PUSH and St. Philip's Episcopal Church Women. Sheila served as Vice President of the Boards of Directors of the YWCA as well as the Girl Scouts of Buffalo and Erie County. She is a founding member of the Black Leadership Forum and currently serves as president of the Western New York M.L. King Commission.

She has received numerous awards for her commitment to human rights, including a citation from Governor Carey; a proclamation from Coleman Young; citations from the County and City of Buffalo for her community efforts; awards from the SUNY Affirmative Action Advisory Council; the American Association for Affirmative Action; the Black Leadership Forum; the Black Educators Association; the AKA Award of acknowledgment for her involvement in global issues; the outstanding service award from the Black Faculty and Staff Association at Buffalo State College; the National Alliance of Black School Educators Award of Meritorious Service and as the National Association of Negro Business and Professional Women's Club's National Award for Meritorious Service.

Sheila has been listed in *Who's Who in America* for five years and when asked about her philosophy, she explained that, "Our family has a tradition of service. We were taught that when you are fortunate, you must give something back. I have been very fortunate because I learned the joy of giving at an early age. The more I have given, the more I've received. I'm a wealthy woman - not in dollars, but in what really counts. Each of us, as individuals, can make a difference. I believe we are really better than we believe and behave. Peace, Love and Progress, Always."

Alrene Olden

Arlene G. Robinson Olden was a native Buffalonian, who was born on April 1, 1937. Her parents were the late Harold and Gladys (Norwood) Robinson. Arlene graduated from Buffalo Public School #47 and East High School. After graduation, she attended E.J. Meyer Memorial Hospital School of Nursing and Millard Fillmore College. She worked at the Buffalo Psychiatric Center and for the Buffalo Board of Education until 1975. Following a period of time during which she worked with her husband Frank, she returned to work with the Federal Civil Service Department as an examiner.

Arlene and Frank were married in 1963. She was the proud and devoted mother of son Kent and grandmother of Kent, Kyle and Kendra. Her family and friends describe her as a meticulous and hard worker, who was never too busy to give help and encouragement to all who needed it. She was an accomplished seamstress, avid reader and traveler. Arlene was an active member of Metropolitan United Methodist Church, where she served on the Disciples Usher Board.

Arlene was the great-grandniece of Harriet Tubman and worked tirelessly to honor the memory of this African American heroine. As one of the founding members of the Harriet Tubman 300's, Arlene was instrumental in many of the accomplishments of this group including placing historical markers at Broderick Park and the Michigan Avenue Baptist Church to mark the Underground Railroad. The organization also was responsible for getting a section of Michigan Avenue renamed "The Harriet Tubman Way" and for the planting of a memorial tree on Harriet Tubman Way. Arlene served as president of the club for two years. She received countless commendations from the city and other organizations in recognition of her work.

Clara L. Payne

Clara L. Payne was a member of an old established Buffalo family. She was born about 1860. She was an active member of Buffalo's small African American community and was very involved with a local civic group that organized, among other activities, a hospitality event for African Americans visiting the 1901 Pan American Exposition. Ms. Payne was listed as one of the members of the Progressive Club's host committee. A local newspaper account of the club's party commended the group for an elaborate and festive gathering that was attended by many visitors to the Exposition.

During World War I, Ms. Payne served as a volunteer nurse at the Marine Hospital in Buffalo during the influenza epidemic of 1917 and 1918. Ms. Payne was employed in several jobs, including positions as a domestic and as a caterer. However, by 1925 she was a social worker and is reported to have been the first African American to work in Erie County's Social Welfare Department. She was described as a dedicated worker who retired from the Welfare Department following a 32-year career.

Her involvement in community organizations was unprecedented. She was a founding member of the Board of Directors of the Buffalo Urban League and remained involved with that organization from 1927 until her death in 1958. A member of the Board of the Young Women's Christian Association (YWCA), Ms. Payne helped to start the first integrated YWCA in the Buffalo area. Ms. Payne's interest in and devotion to the welfare of young women was also expressed through her volunteer work as a Girl Scout Troop leader. Ms. Payne was also a long-time member and officer in the Buffalo Chapter of the NAACP.

Ms. Payne was a member of St. Philip's Episcopal Church where she founded the St. Mary's Guild, the Women's Day worship services and the church's annual Coronation Ball. She also served as a member of the Altar Guild.

Upon learning of her death, on September 5, 1958, the Buffalo Urban League Board passed a resolution that concluded: "Among her many virtues there were integrity, tact, gentleness, a delightful sense of humor; and patience. One can hardly do justice to a characterization of Miss Payne unless she is described as a saint who temporarily sojourned on earth."

Tanya Perrin-Johnson

Tanya received her B.S. from Syracuse University and her M.S. Ed. from Canisius College. She started her career as a fourth-grade teacher at St. Columba School. She then worked as a counselor for Transitional Services, an independent living program for individuals diagnosed with mental illness. Later, she worked with the employment and training division within the Clarkson Center (formerly Allentown Youth Services).

Tanya is currently the Chief Executive Officer of the YWCA of Western New York, Buffalo's oldest and largest organization for women. Since her appointment in 1998, the YWCA of Western New York has expanded its services and programs, adding two Early Childhood Centers, an Apprenticeship Program for teens, the Progressive Adolescent Vocational Exploration Program, the Food Service Training Program, two Children Centers to provide drop-in childcare at Buffalo City Court, Buffalo Employment and Training Center, Universal Pre-K Programs, a "new" Leader Luncheon format which recognizes the achievements of women in Western New York, the I Speak Out -Issue Advocacy Forum, Transitional Housing Units in Amherst and the Women Leaders in Progress Institute.

Before assuming leadership at the YWCA of Western New York, Tanya worked in many capacities at the Clarkson Center, beginning as the Life Skills Educator and later as the Assistant Director of the Employment and Training Division. At the Clarkson Center, Tanya was an advocate for the rights of women and young girls in the workplace.

Tanya understands the importance of community service and serving as a role model for young women. She is a former Board member of Hospice Buffalo, Homespace, Inc., Leadership Buffalo and

Strive for Women. She also served as the YWCA Northeast Regional Representative, the YWCA of the USA Reorganization Task Force.

She currently serves on several boards including: Child Care Coalition, Erie County Commission on the Status of Women (Secretary), Friendship Baptist Church, Mental Health Association (Assistant Secretary), National Association of YW Executives, Not-For-Profit Resource Center and Tapestry Charter School (Vice President). She is a member of Alpha Kappa Alpha Sorority, Inc., Gamma Phi Omega Chapter; Business and Professional Women, Buffalo Chapter; the Erie County Chapter of The Links, Incorporated; Jack and Jill of America, Inc.; National Association of Business Women Owners; Rotary Club of Buffalo and the United Way CEO Institute Advisory Council. She is co-chair of the Asset Building Coalition, co-chair of the United Way Buffalo Region Campaign and the Junior League Community Advisory Council.

Tanya has received numerous awards and recognitions including; Alpha Kappa Alpha Sorority, Inc.; Blazing New Trails in Business Award; Athena Award Nominee; Business First's Forty Under 40 Award; Calvary CME Church, Lifting Extraordinary Women Award; and the National Organization of Women, Women Who Have Made a Difference in Western New York Award. In 2003, she received the Joan A. Levine award from WomanFocus.

Tanya and her husband Charles, reside in Buffalo with their two daughters Cydney and Taylor. Tanya is able to be involved in the many activities due to a supportive family and the strength, perseverance and belief in God. The Johnson family attends Friendship Baptist Church.

Jannie M. Peterson

Jannie M. Peterson received both a B.A. degree in Psychology and a Master of Social Work at the University at Buffalo. Currently, she is a retired Social Work Supervisor for the Erie County Department of Social Services.

Ms. Peterson is the longest standing member of St. John Baptist Church where she serves on the Board of Trustees. In addition, she has served for more than 20 years as a Sunday School Teacher at the Church.

Over the years, Ms. Peterson has given her time to serve on many boards and committees. She currently serves on the Board of the McCarley Gardens Housing Complex. She was a former member of the Governor's Commission on Domestic Violence, the New York State Office for Aging-Older Americans Act Advisory Committee and the Professional and Technical Advisory Committee of Coordinated Care Management Corporation (CCMC). Ms. Peterson also was a former Board member of the Niagara Frontier Association for Sickle Cell Disease, Inc. and volunteered for many years as a Red Cross Ombudsman.

She is affiliated with several prestigious social organizations and is a Life Member of the NAACP as well a Golden Soror of the Alpha Kappa Alpha Sorority, Inc. She is an active member of the Buffalo Chapter of The Links, Incorporated, Harriet Tubman 300's and the Humboldt Bridge Club.

Ms. Peterson has been married for over 60 years to King W. Peterson. They have two children, Lawrence H. and Lorraine P. Rue, four grandchildren and one great-grandchild.

Mary E. Randolph

Mary E. Randolph served for thirty-two years as the Director of Bethel Head Start Program in Western New York, serving low income pre-school children. In 1966 she wrote a proposal for Head Start that was funded in 1967 for $152,000 to serve 133 children in two locations in Buffalo. Under Mrs. Randolph's leadership, this program expanded to serve 575 children and a budget of $3,442,000 in thirteen different locations in Buffalo, Depew, Amherst, Cheektowaga, and Bowmansville. Through her skillful negotiations she guided this program through many collaborations and partnerships with a staff of 102 employees and numerous volunteers. To name a few: Collaboration with Buffalo Public School Even Start, Universal Pre-K, Erie 1 BOCES, State funded Pre-K, Gateway Therapeutic Pre-K, and Summit Academy. These collaborations support the parents by providing training for job preparation and extending the day to provide child care to allow parents to work or attend school.

She secured funds to add a center-based health clinic at the Michigan Avenue site, the only one of its kind nationally. The clinic provides medical care to children in Head Start. In 1993, Mrs. Randolph led her staff in coordinating more than 200 volunteers to build the first community constructed playground in the City of Buffalo that was completed in a single day.

A native of South Carolina, Mrs. Randolph is a graduate of Allen University, Columbia, South Carolina and she received her Masters degree from Buffalo State College. Prior to joining Bethel Head Start she was a primary teacher in the Buffalo Public School System. Mrs. Randolph is a child advocate and believes in giving back to the community. This belief is demonstrated by her membership on many boards, including: Kaleida Health Board of Directors, Chairperson of Human Resources; Summit Academy School Board; King Urban Life Center Board of Directors; The Buffalo Chapter of The Links, Incorporated, Chairperson of Service to Youth; Leadership Buffalo Class of 1989; Alpha Kappa Alpha Sorority, Inc.; Council member

Emeritus SUNY at Buffalo; Law Enforcement and Diversity (LEAD Team) and the National Conference for Community and Justice.

She is also the recipient of numerous awards for her community service including: the University at Buffalo President's Medal, Black Achievers in Industry, Four Chaplains Legion of Honor Award, Region II Head Start Association, H.O.M.E. Director's Award, Brotherhood and Sisterhood Award from the National Conference for Community and Justice, Outstanding Service Award SUNY at Buffalo, AKA Life Long Learning Award, Woman of the Year Zeta Phi Beta Sorority, Jamaican American Association Outstanding Service Award, The Buffalo News 1999 Citizen of the Year, YMCA Toast of Buffalo Award, and the Head Start Award of Excellence.

She is married to Thomas Randolph and the mother of Kimberly and Toinette. Kimberly is a teacher in the Buffalo Public Schools and Toinette is a Special Assistant Attorney General. Mrs. Randolph is a member of Bethel A.M.E. Church and the church serves as Delegate Agency for the Bethel Head Start Program.

Rita Hubbard-Robinson, J.D.

Rita is a graduate of the University at Buffalo Law School and received a Jurisdoctor Degree. She completed undergraduate work at the State University at Binghamton, Harpur College where she earned a Bachelor of Arts Degree majoring in history. She is currently the Executive Director of the Commission on Citizens' Rights and Community Relations for the City of Buffalo and has held this position since 2000. In this position she is responsible for the administration of the human rights commission, an eleven-member group of volunteers. She previously served as the Executive Director of Preventionfocus, Inc., a community-based agency that served more than 20,000 constituents, including parents, women, adolescents and children.

Prior to Preventionfocus, Rita held positions as the Project Director of the University at Buffalo School, College, University Partnership Program; Associate Director of the University at Buffalo

Liberty Partnership Program; Executive Director of the New York State Assembly, Urban Revitalization Task Force; Community Educator and Instructor at the University at Buffalo Institute for CBO Education and Training; Academic Coordinator at the University at Buffalo, Educational Opportunity Program; and Administrative Assistant at the University at Buffalo Learning Center.

Rita is an active community volunteer serving as a member of the Resource Council; Chair, Human Development Committee of the Fruitbelt Task Force; Board Member of the Survivor's Break the Silence; and Langston Hughes Cultural Institute, Development Team member. Past memberships include: Parent Member of the Olmsted School-Based Management Team; Coordinator of Concerned Citizen's Against Violence Coalition; Board member of Housing Assistance Center; the Langston Hughes Cultural Institute; Bethel Head Start and Special Admission Committee, Faculty of Law and Jurisprudence. She also served as the coordinator of the Issues Convention, Uplifting African American Male Youth in 1989 and was an advisor/trainer for the Parent's Committee for an Effective Education.

She is a recipient of the YWCA Executive Award, June 2000; *Who's Who Among Business Executives* and *Who's Who Among Students in American Universities and Colleges*. She has partnered with numerous community groups and organizations, e.g., the Sister to Sister Conference for teenage girls to promote community betterment and empowerment of young people.

Dawn E. Sanders

Dawn is a graduate of the Public Policy and Urban Studies Program at the University at Buffalo where she earned a BA in 1990. She attended the University at Buffalo Micro MBA Program in 1997 and the Harvard Business School Club of Buffalo, Executive Development Program in 1998. In 1999 Dawn enrolled in University at Buffalo, Executive MBA Program. This intensive program selected 36 top executives from the area for a 22-month educational experience.

Dawn E. Sanders is currently employed by the United States Department of Housing and Urban Development (HUD) as a Community Builder. In this position Ms. Sanders works with municipalities and communities on a myriad of housing and economic development and grant programs provided by HUD. Prior to the HUD position, Buffalo City Mayor Anthony Masiello appointed Ms. Sanders to head the Office of Citizen Participation and Information (OCPI) in February 1998. This office was responsible for oversight of the review process for federally funded Community Development Block Grants. In addition, Ms. Sanders' responsibilities included: monitoring and contract compliance of the city's Community Based Organizations and building a comprehensive easy to use application for all of the federally funded programs offered by the City of Buffalo.

Ms. Sander's resume also includes positions as Executive Director of the Office of Urban Initiative, Inc., where she worked to assist minority and women owned business in securing contracts through the County of Erie. As the Executive Director of Citizen Action of New York's Buffalo Regional Office, she worked to improve and advocate for change concerning the environment, health care and the electoral process.

Ms. Sanders received the *40 Under Forty Award from Business First* in 1997. The same year the Southern Christian Leadership Conference also recognized her with an award for Outstanding Community Service. In July 1998 she was the WBLK radio Professional of the

Month. Alpha Kappa Alpha Sorority, Inc. awarded her the Blazing New Trails in Government Award in February 1999.

Ms. Sanders is active in the community. She is the president of Gamma Phi Omega Chapter of Alpha Kappa Alpha Sorority, Inc.; a Board member of the National Conference for Community and Justice; past board member of Gethsemane Foundation and a member of Grassroots, Inc. She is also the first Democratic Party, African American female Zone and Ward Leader.

Rhoda Cornelius Davis Townsend

Rhoda Cornelius Davis Townsend was born in Vincent, Arkansas on March 29, 1902, to Fanny and Thomas Davis.

Her family moved to Wynne, Arkansas in 1912. Rhoda became a Christian at the age of twelve, and was baptized by Dr. W.F. Lovelace at the First Baptist Church. She joined the Junior Choir and was Secretary of the Sunday School.

In 1922, she graduated from Wynne Normal High School. On June 27 of that same year she married Welton Townsend and they moved to Chicago, Illinois. While in Chicago she joined the Pilgrim Baptist Church under the pastorate of S.E.J. Watson.

In 1923, she came to Buffalo and joined the Michigan Avenue Baptist Church, then under the leadership of Dr. J. Edward Nash. She served as president of the Missionary Society and organized the Golden Deeds Club in 1934. She sang in the Choir and was one of three women appointed to the Trustee Board by Dr. Nash in 1935. She served as secretary of the Trustee Board serving three chairmen: Edward Howard, Mason Alexander, and John Harris. She was a faithful member of the Sunday School and served as Secretary, Superintendent, and Teacher of the Women's Class. Mrs. Townsend was a founding member of the Mary B. Talbert Civic and Cultural Club. In addition, she served as President of the Civic Adoration of Women's Clubs, Buffalo Region for eight years. She was a member of the Lit-Mus Study Club beginning in 1928 and served as President,

Secretary, and Treasurer. She was also a member of the Book Lover's Club since 1929, serving as President, Secretary and Treasurer.

Mrs. Townsend died on October 18, 1982 after a long illness.

Joan (Ridley) Willis

Joan Ridley Willis is a retired Social Worker, School Administrator, and Community Activist. She was born in Newport News, Virginia to Hannibal William and Ruth (Spruill) Ridley. She attended the Stockbridge School and obtained a B.A. from the University of Toledo, an M.S.W. from Smith College School of Social Work, a C.A.S. from the State University of New York at Brockport, and completed advanced study at Smith College/Harvard University.

She married the Honorable Charles L. Willis (div) and has one son, Christopher Hannibal and a stepdaughter, Lisa M. Willis.

Ms. Willis has worked as a caseworker, Monroe County Department of Social Services; Clinical Instructor, University of Rochester Medical Center, Department of Psychiatry; Consultant, Genesee Hospital Mental Health Center; Social Worker, Assistant Director and Supervising Director, Pupil Personnel Services; Supervising Director Student Equity and Placement and Supervising Director, Student Support Services/Special Education, Rochester City School District.

Her past and present professional affiliations include: Pi Gamma Mu National Honor Society; New York State School Social Workers; Association of Black Social Workers; National Association of Social Workers; Academy of Certified Social Workers; Monroe County Pupil Services Administrators; New York State Association of Pupil Personnel Administrators, President; National Association of Pupil Services Association; New York State Congress of School Administrators Organization, President; Certified Social Worker, New York State and Phi Delta Kappa International.

Ms. Willis' past and present community affiliations include: Alpha Kappa Alpha Sorority, Inc.; Rochester Community Players; Legal Aid Society, Board of Directors; Rochester Children's Nursery, Board of

Directors; Junior League of Rochester; Jack and Jill of America, Inc.; St. John's Home, Board of Directors; University of Rochester Medical Center, Board of Managers; YWCA, Board of Directors; Monroe County Board of Health, Chair Institutional Review, President; United Way; American Cancer Society; Grief Resource Network; United Nations Association of Rochester and the Rochester Chapter of The Links, Incorporated.

Mary E. Wood

Mary E. Wood was born August 28, 1902 in Des Moines, Iowa to Emmett and Rose Wood. She was educated in the Des Moines Public School System where she graduated from East High School. In 1924 she received her Bachelors Degree from Drake University and continued her education at New York University in New York City, receiving a Master of Arts in Education. In 1968 she received her certification as a Social worker for the state of Pennsylvania.

Mary Wood was the first black woman to hold the position of Executive Director at the YWCA in Buffalo and Erie County. After leaving Buffalo, she held similar positions in several other states. Before retiring in 1972, she was employed as Executive Director for the YWCA of Greater Pittsburgh, Pennsylvania. She served as a consultant for the National Board of the YWCA after her retirement. While serving as consultant for the National Board she implemented their imperative to "eliminate racism anywhere it exists by any means necessary." She also was consultant for World YWCA and was assigned to the Bahamas to upgrade their programs. After Mary retired she became a speaker for various civic groups.

Over the years, she received many honors and accomplishments. In 1924 she was a charter member, Phi Chapter, Delta Sigma Theta Sorority, Inc., a black professional sorority; represented YWCAs of the United States at International Institute, Geneva, Switzerland; Woman of the Year, Zeta Phi Beta, black educational sorority; Medallion, Freedom Foundation at Valley Forge; Outstanding Citizen of New Jersey; Outstanding Community Service Award, Buffalo Urban

League; Good Neighbor Award, Board of Community Relations, Buffalo, New York; Alumni Distinguished Service Award, Drake University; Woman of the Year, Iota Phi Lambda Sorority, Inc.; Distinguished Service Award, USO, Fort Dix, NJ; *Who's Who Among Women in the World;* the Iowa Women Hall of Fame, 1996 and September 4th was designated Mary E. Wood Day in Pittsburgh, PA.

Mary Wood died on November 29, 1998 in Des Moines, Iowa. She was ninety-six years old.

Uncrowned Queens in Education

Carol Hoskins Adams

Carol Hoskins Adams brings more than 35 years of experience as an Educator to her position as Dean of Interdisciplinary Programs at Monroe Community College in Rochester, New York. As a college administrator and Dean, she provides the leadership for several academic programs, services, and departments such as Foreign Languages/ESOL, Transitional Studies, School to College Alliances and the campus Academic Support Services, including the Writing and Tutoring Centers as well as the Writing Across the Curriculum program. She has spearheaded the Teacher Preparation initiative at Monroe Community College. Working in conjunction with the College's Teacher Preparation Advisory Council, she has forged the creation of the Teacher Preparation office as well as three new degree programs and services for future teachers.

In addition, Carol Hoskins Adams has chaired the College's Faculty Orientation Committee where she led the Faculty Development Seminar Series for several years. She has presented at national conferences for the League for Innovation, the National Institute of Staff and Organizational Development, the Community College Humanities Association and the National Association of Developmental Education. As part of her professional development, she has completed the Cornell University, Academic Leadership Program through the Institute for Community College Development in their Department of Education in Ithaca, New York.

Carol received the SUNY Chancellor's Award for Excellence in Professional Service, the Rochester City School District's Women's History Month Award, MCC Most Distinguished Professor's Award for Professional Services and the American Association of Women in Community and Junior College's Award for the National Institute of Leadership Development.

In the community, Carol has served on the United Way's African American Leadership Development Steering Committee, the University of Rochester's Advisory Board for the Youth and Family Project, the YWCA's Board of Directors and is currently serving on Planned Parenthood's Rochester, Syracuse Regional Board of Directors.

Carol Hoskins Adams holds a Bachelor of Arts degree in Education from Michigan State University and a Master of Science degree from Queens College, City University of New York.

Anna Porter Burrell

Dr. Anna Porter Burrell was born in Philadelphia in 1902. She graduated from high school and a two-year Normal School before completing a Bachelor of Science in chemistry from the University of Pennsylvania in 1923. Dr. Burrell's teaching career in higher education began at Lincoln University in Jefferson City, Missouri, where she taught chemistry from 1923-25.

In 1926, she earned a Master of Science degree in Medical Sciences from her alma mater, the University of Pennsylvania. She was one of 81 women to receive a Master's degree in a class of nearly 300. Dr. Burrell's career path took her to Howard University in Washington, D.C., where she taught bacteriology. She also met her future husband, Robert Burrell at Howard.

In 1945, Dr. Burrell enrolled in the doctoral program in psychology and human relations at New York University. Dr. Burrell came to Buffalo to teach at Buffalo State College in 1948. She was the first African American faculty member to be hired by the College. Her husband, Robert was an attorney in the Buffalo District Attorney's office. He later became a City Court Judge. Dr. Burrell's interest in child development, human relations and international education led to her involvement in education in India. In 1959, she received a Fulbright Fellowship to study at Jabalpu University in India. This was followed by an appointment to the post of Director of the India Project at Buffalo State that resulted in several trips with students, in 1968-69 and 1970-71, to study the educational system and culture of that country. She was also the College's Director of Human Relations Workshops. Dr. Burrell retired from Buffalo State in 1972.

Dr. Burrell was an active member of the Committee for World Affairs and World Hospitality Association. She also was involved in several other community organizations. She was honored by numerous groups, including: B'Nai B'Rith, National Conference for

Community and Justice; the University at Buffalo and the Urban League. Dr. Burrell lectured throughout the United States on Labor, Children, and Discrimination, and in addition, published several articles. Dr. Burrell died in 1981. The Dr. Anna P. Burrell Underrepresented Minority Scholarship Fund was established in her honor.

Pauline Winifred Huff Byrd

Pauline Winifred Huff was born December 23, 1908, to Rev. General Grant Huff and Junior Wilson Huff, in New Market, Tennessee. Pauline received her early education in Greenville, South Carolina. In 1932 she earned a B.A. degree from Livingstone College in Salisbury, North Carolina. She pursued graduate studies at Buffalo State College during the early 1960s. This foundation prepared her for 19 years of employment as an elementary education teacher for the Buffalo Board of Education at Public Schools 6, 38, and 48. While a student at Livingstone, she was a charter member of the local undergraduate chapter of Alpha Kappa Alpha Sorority, Inc.

Pauline's journey as the quiet, calm, loyal mate to a preacher of the Gospel began at St. James A.M.E. Zion Church in Ithaca, New York in 1933. Pauline and her husband, the Reverend Derrick M. Byrd, Sr., moved to Buffalo a few years later. This ministry led to experiences at St. Luke A.M.E. Zion Church of Buffalo in 1936 and charter membership at People's Church, founded by Rev. Byrd in 1938. During her work at People's, which spanned 50 years, she served as pianist, organist, director of the Senior and Junior choirs and the Minister of Music. In addition, Pauline taught piano and voice lessons to many Buffalo area residents, while she studied organ under the tutelage of Muriel Davidson, and was presented in recital at St. Paul's Cathedral in Buffalo.

Mrs. Byrd's other church and community affiliations included membership in the Missionary Society and the Community Church Club of People's Church, delegate to the organizing conference of the National Council of Community Churches at Lake Forest, Illinois in

1950, Church Women United (World Day of Prayer), Wider Horizons Reading Program; Leukemia Society volunteer, Meals on Wheels,Buffalo Urban League and American Association for Retired Persons (AARP) .

Rev. and Mrs. Byrd were the proud parents of two sons, Derrick, Jr. and Cameron, Sr.; grandchildren, Cameron, Jr., Brian, Jeannine, Pamela, Kahlil, Derria; and one great-grandchild, Andre. Mrs. Byrd died on December 18, 1989, a few days before her eighty-first birthday.

Delores E. Coleman

Delores E. Coleman was born in Chicago, Illinois and moved to Buffalo in 1977 with her husband and childhood sweetheart, Stanley Coleman, also a native of Chicago. A graduate of Parker High School in Chicago, Delores continued her education in Buffalo completing several certificate and degree programs, including: Teaching Certification, Buffalo Research Institute on Education for Teaching, the University at Buffalo, 1995; M.A., American Studies/Black Feminists, University at Buffalo, 1992; B.A., American Studies/Women's Studies, University at Buffalo, 1986; National Seminars, Inc. Workshop, Powerful Business Writing Skills, and Careertrack, Management and Leadership Skills for Women.

Delores is a Social Studies teacher and member of the Learning Standards and Curriculum Department for the Buffalo Public Schools. Delores and Stan are co-owners of Appaloosa Video Productions, LTD. Since 1988, the couple has recorded the video histories of many community and church organizations.

Delores' community involvement is mirrored in the many organizations and groups that she actively participates in such as: Founding member, 50 Women with a Vision, a group of women committed to restoring Jefferson Avenue in Buffalo to a business and shopping district; Member of Alpha Kappa Alpha Sorority, Inc., Xi Epsilon Omega Chapter; Member, Pan Hellenic Council, Western New York; Former Member, Phi Lambda Theta-Alpha Nu Chapter;

Educational Tutor, Women for Human Rights and Dignity, Inc.; Board of Directors, Alleyway Theater; Past President and member of the Board of Directors, Inner City Ballet; Advisory Board Member, United Negro College Fund; a past Woman of the Year and Historian, American Business Women's Association, Frontier Chapter; Coalition of 100 Black Women, Buffalo Chapter; Nia Writer's Workshop, Langston Hughes Cultural Institute and Fundraising Chairperson, Hot Ice Ski Club.

Delores and Stan are the proud parents of Stella and Angela, and grandparents of Bria, Aaliyah, Mya, and Dwight Jr. Delores also has two older sisters, Maudell Walton of Chicago, Illinois; Eurina Bundy of New York, New York and a brother, Vermon Dright, Jr. of St. Paul, Minnesota.

Delores has been a member of Jordan Grove Baptist Church, Buffalo, since 1990.

Donnie Duke

Donnie Duke moved to Buffalo with her family in the late 1920's. She attended the Buffalo Public Schools and graduated from Hutchinson Central High School with many honors and the coveted Jeanie Gunson Award. She was offered six scholarships to attend college and picked a work-study scholarship to the University at Buffalo, where she later earned a Bachelor's degree in Sociology and Anthropology with a minor in Psychology. She attended graduate school in Social Work and upon graduation was immediately hired by the Erie County Department of Social Services where she worked for over thirty-five years as a supervisor. Following her retirement, Ms. Duke took a position with the Educational Opportunity Center at the University at Buffalo where she was a popular instructor who taught many seminars on African American History.

As an avocation, she became an avid bridge player and teacher. She was a Life Master in the American Bridge Association in which she won many tournaments and trophies.

Ms. Duke was one of the founding members of the Gamma Kappa Chapter of Delta Sigma Theta Sorority, Inc.

Prior to her death on March 26, 2002, Donnie Duke volunteered in the Office of Black Ministry in the Diocese of Buffalo, where she made tapes on ministries and Christian heraldry explaining the Church Symbols.

Ms. Duke is sister to another Uncrowned Queen, Eva Noles.

Catherine Eberhart

Catherine Eberhart was born and raised in Buffalo, New York. She lived in the Willert Park Projects for her first 7 years and an almost daily visit to the Willert Park Library helped her develop a love for reading. Currently, Catherine is an English Teacher at Lincoln Academy #44. A graduate, BS and MS in Education, of Buffalo State College, she has been teaching since 1972. In her early teaching career, she spent 10 years at the Diocesan Educational Campus.

Volunteering has been a way of life for Catherine. As a teenager, Catherine began volunteering for the YWCA. During her college years she became active in local human service organizations and served as Secretary/Treasurer for Ellicott Human Services Association for 25 years. Her association with Juneteenth Festival, Inc. started in the early 1980's and she is still serving as Treasurer. She is also Secretary of the Greater Buffalo Soap Box Derby. For the past 20 years, Catherine has been on the planning committee for the East High School Class of 1968 reunions.

Aside from teaching, Catherine works part-time in the business world. She has held part-time bookkeeping jobs and was a Sarah Coventry Jewelry Sales Rep. In 1980 she started a tax preparation service for small businesses and individuals. Catherine plans to continue operating this service when she retires from teaching. Since 1993, she has been studying aromatherapy and recently started a home-based business selling holistic health products. She is currently in training to be a Natural Health Consultant with a focus on aromatherapy.

Estella Norwood Evans

Dr. Estella Norwood Evans, CSW, ACSW, Founding Director of the Greater Rochester Collaborative MSW Program and Professor of Social Work at Nazareth College of Rochester, has been a member of the Nazareth faculty since 1981. She chaired the Social Work Department from 1987 to 1997. She relinquished her role as Chair of the Social Work Department to develop the new MSW Program. This marks the first collaborative graduate MSW Program in the country between a private college and a public university, which recently achieved Candidacy status, the final phase in the initial accreditation process by the Council on Social Work Education. In January 1999 Dr. Norwood Evans was named the 1998-99 Phi Delta Kappa Educator of the Year by the local education fraternity. On the Nazareth College campus, she is a member of the Faculty Diversity Sub-Committee, the Health and Human Services Professions Committee, the Academic Standards Committee, and the MSW Social Work Advisory Committee.

Dr. Norwood Evans previously taught full-time in the Departments of Social Work at SUNY College at Brockport and the Hunter College School of Social Work, City University of New York. Prior to teaching she spent 12 years as a social worker in the New York City and Connecticut areas. She earned her undergraduate degree at the University of Michigan at Ann Arbor, her Masters degree in Social Work at the University of Connecticut, and her Ph.D. at Yeshiva University.

She is a current accreditation site visitor for the Council on Social Work Education, the national social work accrediting body, as well as a site visitor for the New York State Education Department and was recently appointed by the President of the Council on Social Work Education to the CSWE Commission on Racial, Ethnic, and Cultural Diversity. Dr. Norwood Evans is a current member of the Board of Christian Education, a past member of the Board of Trustees, and immediate past Co-Chair of the capital campaign which raised several million dollars to build a new sanctuary at Mt. Olivet Baptist Church in Rochester. Within the community she is a member of the Board of Directors of the American Red Cross - Rochester Chapter, a member of the Board of Directors of Catholic Family Center, a member of the Advisory Committee of the Monroe Community College Human Services Program, and a member of the Advisory Committee of the Lend Grant, and interdisciplinary training grant based at the University of Rochester Medical Center. Her past Board memberships in the Rochester community are extensive and include: the National Association of Social Workers, Genesee Valley Division as past elected delegate (two terms) to the Delegate Assembly, the national elected policy making body of NASW, Chair of the Legislative Committee, and Division Representative to the State Board, past Board Member of The Legal Aid Society, Rochester Children's Nursery, Asbury Child Care Center, Hillside Children's Center St. Joseph's Villa, the Baden Street Settlement Counseling Center, and the Southeast YMCA. She has published and delivered lectures, presentations, and workshops worldwide on social work and diversity issues in such countries as Israel, Peru, the Netherlands and Ghana, West Africa.

During the summer of 1999, Dr. Norwood Evans received the prestigious honor of representing the Greater Rochester Community of Churches, a city wide ecumenical body, on the interfaith team selected to study at the Yad Vashem International School for Holocaust Studies in Jerusalem, Israel. She continues to provide lectures, workshops and presentations as a holocaust educator in the greater Rochester community.

Dr. Norwood Evans was the 1995 recipient of the Rochester Community Service Award presented by the Tribute to Great Women Committee of the Rochester Community and she was a Ford Foundation National Fellow. She was the 1999 recipient of the Nazareth College Martin Luther King Jr. Award. Additionally, Dr. Norwood Evans was recently appointed by Mayor William Johnson to serve on his Commission on Race and Ethnic Relations for the greater Rochester community. Most recently Dr. Norwood Evans was nominated to serve on the New York State Education Department Board of Regents.

Rita Fraiser

Rita E. Fraiser is a Buffalo native, and has dedicated her life to developing and expanding the minds of young children for the past 26 years. Believing throughout her career as both teacher and administrator that "Together we can make a difference," Rita has focused on giving her all to the field of education both inside and outside of the classroom.

After receiving her Bachelor of Science degree in Secondary Education Biology in 1975, Rita began her career within the educational community teaching elementary science at the Diocesan Educational Campus School from 1975-1984. Realizing that she could not continue to expand the minds of our youth without first expanding her own, Rita returned to school and received her Master's Degree of Science in Secondary Education from Canisius College in 1982. Upon completion of her Master's Degree, Rita, faced with the new responsibility of raising a family of her own, decided to leave the classroom and take a brief sabbatical to focus her energies on developing the minds of her own children. Rita raised three successful children, Shniece - Regional Manager, Charles Jr. - Naval Officer, and Levar - Engineer.

With the strong desire to bring her motto to fruition, Rita returned to the classroom in 1989 as both a teacher and student. She joined the Buffalo Board of Education as a science teacher, but she knew that she could give more if she moved out of the classroom and into administration. Therefore, she decided to attend Canisius College to obtain a Masters of Science in Educational Administration/ Supervisor Certification. Within the Buffalo Board of Education, first as a teacher and as an administrator over the past five years, Rita has held various positions such as, Liberty Partnership Coordinator, Magnet School Specialist and Math Coordinator; Acting Assistant Principal, Futures Academy and Assistant Principal, Emerson High School. Rita has moved quickly through the ranks becoming well-known as a shining star who could master any task or obstacle placed within her path.

Rita became Principal of Stanton Academy (P.S. #31) and is presently Principal of BUILD Academy where she lives her motto on a daily basis, "Together we can make a difference."

Rita has many interests such as golfing, swimming, and traveling. She has visited many places such as the Far East, Europe, and Japan.

Rita is an active member of the Association for Supervision/ Curriculum Development, Middle Level Association, Phi Delta Kappa and Metropolitan Buffalo Alliance of Black School Educators. She has been an active member of Alpha Kappa Alpha Sorority, Inc. for twenty-six years, holding several officer positions in Xi Epsilon Omega Chapter. Rita was recently elected as the group's president.

Danis Gehl

Danis Joyce Gehl is the Project Director, University Community Initiative (UCI), a public service project directed toward stabilizing and improving the neighborhoods surrounding the Main Street Campus of the University at Buffalo. Ms. Gehl has spent most of her professional life working in the housing and human services fields. Much of her work has been with block clubs and other grassroots neighborhood organizations. She was the Executive Director of Kensington Bailey Neighborhood Housing Services, the Director of the Family Advocacy Program for Child and Family Services, and the Neighborhood Services Coordinator for the Community Planning Assistance Center of Western New York.

Throughout Ms. Gehl's membership in many neighborhood and community organizations, the development and maintenance of healthy neighborhoods has remained a major area of interest. She was the chairperson of the Oversight Committee for the 1993 Buffalo Common Council Housing Preservation Study, was a member of the United Way of Buffalo and Erie County Needs Assessment Committee and served on the board of many community organizations. Ms. Gehl sits on the boards of Child and Family Services, the YWCA of Western New York, and Fidelis Care New

York. She is active in her parish St. Martin de Porres Roman Catholic Church and is a member of the Leadership Buffalo class of 1999.

Recognized for her expertise in the non-profit sector, Ms. Gehl has given presentations, led workshops, seminars or planning sessions for such organizations as Working for Downtown, the Langston Hughes Cultural Institute, Kensington Bailey Neighborhood Housing Services, the American Planning Association (Western New York Chapter), United Neighborhoods, the Roll Call for Racism and the Erie County Council on Children and Families.

Ms. Gehl has been recognized for her work in housing and neighborhood development by numerous organizations including, the Buffalo Common Council, Buffalo Neighborhood Housing Services and Housing Opportunities Made Equal (HOME).

Ms. Gehl received her Bachelor of Arts and Master's degrees from the University at Buffalo where she is currently pursuing a doctorate in Sociology. Ms. Gehl is also lecturer in the UB Millard Fillmore College.

Ernestine R. Green

Ernestine R. Green was born in Queens, New York. She is the daughter of Eugene and Bertha Riddick and is proud to be from a family of seven girls. She came to Buffalo in 1955 to attend Buffalo State Teachers College and graduated in 1959. She returned to Long Island but was unable to work as a teacher in the public school system because it did not welcome minority teachers at that time. Instead she did social work for the Nassau County Department of Welfare. She returned to Buffalo in 1960 and married Justice Samuel Green.

Ms. Green was the First Woman to be appointed to the Niagara Frontier Transportation Authority by the former Governor Hugh Carey in 1980. She was reappointed by former Governor Mario Cuomo in 1987. While at the NFTA, Ms. Green initiated and chaired the Minority Task Force which helps local minority businesses to work with the NFTA to secure contracts. In addition, she initiated and chaired the Art Selection Committee of the NFTA. A million and one-half dollars of public art represented by all members of the community was placed in the seven Metro stations.

Her affiliations have included: Commissioner and Vice Chair, Niagara Frontier Transportation Authority; Trustee, Statler Foundation; Board of Directors and Chair - Strategic Board Placement Committee, Leadership Buffalo; Board of Trustees, Medaille College; Founder, Chair - Renaissance Women; Co-chair, Ebony and Ivory Ball Fund Raiser; Member, The Women's Group - Professional Women Coming Together to Network and Address Concerns of Women on all Issues; Member, Leadership Buffalo Class of '92; Buffalo Urban League; Buffalo Chapter NAACP and Board of Trustees, Buffalo State College Foundation.

Former community affiliations include: Founder, Black Educators Association; Founder and Board Member, St Philips Boys and Young Men's Choir; First Woman to be Appointed to the Niagara Frontier Transportation Authority; Founder and Chair of Women for Gorski; Chair, Educational Committee of the Buffalo Philharmonic Orchestra and others.

Ms. Green and her husband have one daughter, Beth, who is a practicing attorney in Forest Hills, New York.

Carlita Jones

The Muse of History records immortal queens as leaders. There are those who lead ostentatiously and boldly...and those who lead subtly, quietly, and discreetly while helping to mold a strong future for an appreciative people, a fortunate spouse, and aspiring heirs.

Carlita Murphy Jones must be remembered in the latter category of uncrowned queens. She was born in Baltimore, Maryland of nationally renowned parents, Dr. Carl Murphy, a NAACP Spingarn Medal awardee and President of the one hundred year old Afro-American Newspaper, and Vashti Turley Murphy, Co-founder of Delta Sigma Theta Sorority, Inc. She has been sharing those bequeathed gifts with those in Buffalo for years.

In 1942, Mrs. Jones earned a BA in Journalism from the University of Wisconsin. She also holds an MS in Education from the University at Buffalo (1964).

For more than 30 years, Mrs. Jones took extra delight in teaching children in the Buffalo Public Schools the importance and techniques of reading, writing and using the English language correctly. To this day, she has her own written, unpublished thesaurus, to which she regularly makes additions. She continues to proof-read the writings of her spouse, her children, and friends who unashamedly seek her assistance.

Mrs. Jones is a life member of NAACP, member of Delta Sigma Theta Sorority, Inc. since 1941 and member of The Links, Incorporated since 1967.

She has been married for over 58 years to Buffalo's first Black Council member, Rev. Leeland N. Jones, Jr., who is the Associate Pastor of Bethel AME Church. The Reverend and Mrs. Jones have three children: Dr. Leeland AM Jones, Sr. M.D.; Atty. Johnaaron M. Jones, Esquire; and Mrs. Carlita CMJ Perkins, Sr. Executive Vice President, Success Results Consulting, Inc. in Germantown, Maryland.

Rowena Adams Jones

Rowena Adams Jones is a retired Professional Administrator at the University at Buffalo, (UB) for 26 years. She was born in Johnstown, Pennsylvania and graduated from Johnstown Senior High School and later attended the University of Pittsburgh where she received a BA in Elementary Education in 1950. She received her Master's Degree in Education at the University at buffalo in 1972.

While at UB, Mrs. Adams Jones created and developed the Browsing Library Study Centers for all students in the Residence Halls. She coordinated the University Friendship 101 Program for all Freshmen, and co-taught a course on mentoring for Cora P. Maloney College. She is the recipient of many honors at UB including the Professional Staff Outstanding Service Award, Outstanding Service to University at Buffalo Minority

Faculty and Staff Association, SUNY Outstanding Award for Professional Staff and the Appreciation Award for Dedicated Service to the Black Student Union.

Mrs. Adams Jones has been an active member of St. Luke A.M.E. Zion Church for more than 50 years and was past Christian Education Director, Sunday School Teacher and Director of the Nursery. She is currently President of the Ideal Club and a member of Concerned Parents Council, the Ruby C. Smith Scholarship Committee, the Laity Council, and Missionary Life. She is also the recipient of the Hunter B. Bess Memorial Award for service to God and Zion.

Mrs. Adams Jones has been actively involved in the community throughout her life. She was a Girl Scout Leader of the Buffalo and Erie County Girl Scout Council for over 25 years. She started as a Brownie Leader and advanced through each level with her girls to the Senior level. She served as Chair on the Personnel Committee, Trainer for the Brownies, Phone-a-Thon committee, received an Appreciation Award from the Girl Scout Council and was one of 75 leaders recognized at the 75th Anniversary of Girl Scouting.

Mrs. Adams Jones has been an active member of Delta Sigma Theta Sorority, Inc. for over 50 years. In addition, she is a member of the Buffalo Alumnae Chapter; Co-chair Jabberwock Extravaganza, 1985; Director, Historical Fashion Show by Chapter - presented at Regional and National Conferences of Delta; Recipient of Appreciation Award for Service to Buffalo Alumnae Chapter and the Delta Sigma Theta Sorority, Inc. Award for 50 years of service.

Mary Ruth Kapsiak

Mary Ruth Kapsiak began her career as a NYNEX Corporation Customer Service Representative employed in Business Marketing. She has earned several degrees including a Bachelor of Arts in Speech Communication, University at Buffalo; Certificate of Completion, Orton-Gillingham Method for Reading from Gow School; Master of Science in Exceptional Education, from Buffalo State College; Master of Science, reading, Canisius College and completed school administration supervision certification from Canisius College.

She was a special education teacher and reading teacher at Community School #53 in Buffalo. Prior to her experiences at School #53, Mary Ruth was a reading teacher for grades pre-kindergarten through six at Broadway Village Elementary # 57 where she conducted assessments and evaluations while teaching the Orton-Gillingham method of reading. In September of 2002, Mrs. Kapsiak was appointed Assistant Principal of Stanton Academy #31.

Her professional associations include the following: Membership in Kappa Delta Pi International Honor Society; Member, Metro Buffalo Alliance of Black School Educators; Member, Phi Delta Kappa Professional Organization; Member, Delta Kappa Gamma Society International; Alpha Kappa Alpha Sorority, Inc., Xi Epsilon Omega Chapter; Board of Directors, Women for Human Rights and Dignity: University at Buffalo Alumni Association; Canisius College Alumni and many others.

Her awards and honors are numerous and include: Western New York Educational Leadership Council, 2003; Apple for the Teacher Award, Iota Phi Lambda Sorority, Inc., 1996; NAACP Membership Award, 1986; International Register of Profiles, London, England, 1983; and many more.

Mary Ruth attributes her accomplishments to God and a loving family. She is a member of St. John Baptist Church where she contributes to the Sunday school and Nurses Ministries. She resides in Buffalo with her husband Jim.

Nellie B. King

Nellie B. King was raised in a rural area called Foxworth near Columbia, Mississippi. Her professional career of more than 35 years has centered on school life, serving school communities as a teacher, Elementary School Principal, Principal of Secondary Curriculum and Instruction and Superintendent.

In 1965, Ms. King earned a B.A. degree in Social Studies from Alcorn A and M College in Lorman, Mississippi. Later she earned a Master of Science degree in Education from Canisius College in Buffalo. She obtained a Certificate of Advanced Study in Educational Administration from the University at Buffalo in 1974. In addition, she is certified by the Buffalo State College in Social Studies, School Administration, and Supervision.

During her nine-year tenure as Superintendent of the Lackawanna City School District, Ms. King developed and initiated the Kids in Spotlight Program, Lackawanna Center for Family Achievement and the District Model Aids Program. During the 1998-1999 school year she researched selected School District Strong Arts Education and Humanities Programs across the country for the United State's President's Committee on the Arts and Humanities which resulted in a published report, *Gaining the Arts Advantage.*

On November 19, 1999, she was one of fifteen participants from around the country selected by the Department of Agriculture Office of the Secretary to participate in a roundtable discussion with Shirley R. Watkins, Undersecretary, Food, Nutrition and Consumer Services. Under Ms. King's leadership, the Lackawanna School District initiated new opportunities for student success such as Early Grade Reduced Class Size, 21st Century Community Learning Centers Grant, extended Day/School Violence Prevention and the Gear-up Program.

Her citations and awards include: National Association of Counties Achievement Award; Buffalo Ambassador; Lackawanna Board of Education Excellence Award; Community Award Buffalo Club of National Association of Negro Business and Professional Women's Clubs, Inc.; Edna Seay Founder's Award, Alpha Kappa

Alpha Sorority, Inc.; Bridge Builder's Award, Alpha Kappa Alpha Sorority, Inc.; Personalities in Black History Award; United Negro College Fund Award, Distinguished Leadership; Martin Luther King, Jr. Award for Education; and Outstanding president Alpha Kappa Alpha Sorority, Inc. Great Lakes Region. She was also chosen as one of Buffalo's outstanding Black Women by *The Buffalo Challenger* Editor and received other awards including Outstanding Religious Service by the Council of Churches, Buffalo, New York; Outstanding Principal Award, Black Educators Association of Western New York; Woman of the Year at Calvary C.M.E. Church and Teacher of the Year Award, Lincoln Jr. High School.

Ms. King is an active member in several community and civic organizations including Calvary Christian Methodist Episcopal Church; Alpha, Kappa Alpha Sorority, Inc.; Women's Missionary Council of Christian Methodist Church; World Federation of Methodist Women; Ruth Lightsey Scholarship Program, Calvary CME Church; and the Western New York United Negro College Telethon.

Elmira Mangum

Dr. Mangum received her Ph.D. from the University at Buffalo. She also graduated with honors from the University of Wisconsin-Madison with two master's degrees, one in Public Policy and Public Administration and another in Urban and Regional Planning. But most importantly Dr. Mangum received her foundation and inspiration for service at North Carolina Central University (NCCU), one of the nations historically black colleges and universities, where she graduated magna cum laude with a major concentration in the field of geography. While enrolled at NCCU she served in Washington, DC as the first African American U.S. Congressional Intern from the State of North Carolina. She is also a graduate of the Harvard University Graduate School of Education Management Development Program and the Cornell University Administrative Management Institute. Dr. Elmira

Mangum is currently serving as Associate Provost for Finance and Human Resources at the University of North Carolina, Chapel Hill where she provides administrative leadership that supports the financial, human resources, facilities, and planning issues across the Provostial organization.

A native of North Carolina, Dr. Mangum has held several administrative posts in higher education and management, including the University of Wisconsin-Madison and the University at Buffalo. Immediately before coming to Carolina, at the University at Buffalo, she held the positions of Vice Provost and Associate Provost for Finance. Her history in higher education includes working with students and parents on educational planning through financial management, and she has worked directly with faculty and students in her role as Assistant Dean for Academic Affairs and Financial Management with the School of Management. Throughout her career, she has been involved with manycommunity and statewide committees from coastal and sea grant programs to regional planning initiatives.

Her career has been dedicated to providing leadership and managerial support to all levels within the university and the community from executives, to faculty, to students, to project directors, and national organizations in strategic planning, operations analyses, policy development, systems design and process transformation and implementation. Dr. Mangum has also been more directly involved with students through teaching courses in educational leadership and policy, and student mentoring. She has mentored professional staff as well as managed the Professional Staff Senate internship program at the University of Buffalo.

She was chosen by the American Association of State Colleges and Universities as one of 30 rising leaders from across the United States to participate in the first class of the Millennium Leadership Institute. She successfully completed that program in Washington, D.C. in the summer of 1999. She has served on the program committee of the American Association of Higher Education, Summit on Blacks in Higher Education and is a member of the American Council of Education, Network for Women Leaders in Higher Education.

During her stay in Buffalo, New York she was a founding member of the local chapter of the Auxiliary to the National Medical Association, and member of the Board of Directors of the William

Emslie YWCA. Other professional, social and religious affiliations include the New York State Organization of Bursars and Business Administrators, the Institute for Research on Women and Gender, University at Buffalo; Zeta Phi Beta Sorority; Phi Delta Kappa; United Way of Erie County Investment Board; the Greater Refuge Temple of Christ; the National Association for Equal Opportunity, the National Association of Colleges and University Business Officers; Tudor Book Club and the National Brotherhood of Skiers. Dr. Mangum serves annually as a judge in NAACP ACT-SO competition and is also a member of the National Council of Negro Women.

Her colleagues, the Girl Scout Council of Erie County and other organizations across the country have recognized her work, love for children, and community service through awards, speaking invitations, and planning committees.

Kay E. Martin

Born on August 5, 1932, to James and Ellen Marable of Niagara Falls, New York, Kay Elizabeth Marable was named after her mother's two sisters, Katherine and Elizabeth. She was raised on 13th Street and later in the Center Court Housing Project where she became involved with girl scouting and baseball, among other activities. After attending Center Avenue Elementary and North Junior High Schools, she went on to Niagara Falls High where she was a member of many clubs and organizations including the school band in which she played the bass fiddle.

Kay excelled academically and earned a Regent's diploma and scholarship, which she used to attend Buffalo State College. During this time, she married and began a family. Kay continued to attend college as she single-parented her children: Dawn, James, Denise, David, and Damon.

Kay earned her Bachelor's degree (1957) and a Master's degree (1978) from Buffalo State College. She subsequently earned her Ph.D. from the University at Buffalo in 1984. Throughout her educational endeavors, she worked simultaneously as a local educator. She taught in the Buffalo Public School System for ten years before assuming the position of Coordinator of Academic Affairs of the SEEK Program at Buffalo State College. She also was the Director of Personnel and Affirmative Action for the New York State Office of Mental Health. Following this position, she taught English as an Assistant Professor at Buffalo State College. Kay was the Director of Academic Services at the University at Buffalo from 1983 until her retirement in 1991.

As an educator, she has had a lasting, positive impact on thousands of children. Dr. Martin was known to many of her students as very demanding. Her expectations were set high, but were always delivered with a "mother's love." Over the years, she earned and received many accolades, acknowledgements, and awards including: Woman of the Year from New Hope Baptist Church, Niagara Falls; Director of the Year, Educational Opportunity Program Directors; Outstanding Educator, United University Professionals; Outstanding Educator, Cecil F. Brown Democratic Club and the Rockefeller Scholarship, Rockefeller Foundation.

Kay retired in 1991 to care for and spend time with her terminally ill son, David, who passed away the following year. Since then, she has devoted her time to community-based projects, as well as being "Ma" and "Nana" to her four children, nine grandchildren, and eight great-grandchildren, all of whom adore and admire her greatly.

Johnnie M. Mayo

Johnnie M. Mayo is the oldest of seven children. Her family increased by four when cousins were introduced following the loss of her maternal aunt. As a sixteen-year-old high school student, Johnnie began a continuing commitment to community service. She taught Sunday school and volunteered regularly at the campaign headquarters of various political aspirants.

Her lifelong dream to be a teacher was achieved when she graduated from Buffalo State College in 1959 and began a thirty-seven year career in education. After teaching in various elementary schools Mrs. Mayo became principal of the BUILD Academy in 1970. Her participation in the development of the Academy is one of her proudest accomplishments. Many members of her extended family attended and graduated from the school. Most are now college graduates or are college bound.

In 1985, Johnnie was one of four, and the only female, to be appointed by the Buffalo Board of Education to the position of Supervising Principal. In 1990, she became the first African American female to be promoted to the rank of Assistant Superintendent for elementary Education in the Buffalo Public Schools. She continues, in retirement, to mentor newly appointed administrators, in the public and private sector, throughout the Western New York area.

After retirement from the Buffalo Public School System, Johnnie taught a graduate course in Education at her alma mater, Buffalo State College. In 1983, Johnnie also served as a Project Consultant for the U.S. Department of Education. She offered technical assistance on alternative practices related to the overrepresentation of Black and minority students in classes for the Educable Mentally Retarded. This assistance was provided to school districts throughout the country.

Over the years, Mrs. Mayo has served on numerous organizational boards including Housing Opportunities Made Equal (H.O.M.E.) and the Board of A.D.D.S., a full-service chemical dependency treatment program, which provides emergency, residential, and outpatient rehabilitation services to men, women, and adolescents. Mrs. Mayo is a Board Member and mentor for girls in the BuffaloPrep program. On the Board of Education at Our Savior Lutheran Church, Johnnie is a member of the Scholarship Committee and served as Chair of the church's 75th Anniversary celebration in 2001.

Johnnie has served as president of Alpha Kappa Alpha Sorority, Inc., Gamma Phi Omega chapter, chairperson of the scholarship Committee, Founders Day, and MLK, Jr. program. She presently serves as Protocol chair and is active on many chapter committees. She has been a delegate to national and international sorority conferences. She is a member of Buffalo Chapter of The Links, Incorporated where she has served as vice-president, recording secretary, and is presently the chair of the International Trends and Services committee. A Read Across America participant, Johnnie is actively engaged in reading with, and to, students in schools throughout the Buffalo area.

She is the recipient of numerous awards for community service including: The National Association of Negro Business and Professional Women's Club's Sojourner Truth Award; Alpha Kappa Alpha Sorority, Inc., Gamma Phi Omega's Founders Day Award; National Conference for Community and Justice's Brotherhood/ Sisterhood Award; Dreamers Unlimited Triumph Award for Strength, Wisdom and Perseverance; YWCA Leader Nominee for volunteerism; Alpha Kappa Alpha Sorority, Inc., Gamma Phi Omega's Ouida H. Clapp Distinguished Sisterhood Award and the AKA/Gamma Phi Omega's Spirit of AKA Award.

Johnnie M. Mayo is married to John A. Mayo and is the mother of Michael and Gina Mayo Hawk and the grandmother of five.

Clyde Boddie Murphy

Clyde Wilkins Boddie Murphy, the daughter of the late Dr. and Mrs. Julian Franklin Boddie, was born in Milledgeville, Georgia. She graduated from Eddy High School in Milledgeville then attended West Virginia State College where she received a BA in Elementary Education in 1942. In 1944 she attended Atlanta University where she earned a MA in Social Work and in 1978 she received an Ed.M. in Early Childhood Education from the University at Buffalo.

Clyde married Dr. Benjamin Franklin Murphy in 1945. Dr. Murphy was well known and respected as an excellent and caring physician. During their marriage of 54 years Clyde and Frank were blessed with three children: Clyde Edith, a lawyer; Pamela Elizabeth, a school psychologist; and Benjamin Franklin III, a child protection case manager; and two grandchildren, Damani Benjamin Johnson and Elizabeth Murphy.

Over her career history Clyde Murphy held a number of positions in the social work and education fields. She served as a social worker helping pregnant teenagers at the Salvation Army Booth Memorial Hospital. She held a position at the University at Buffalo, School of Nursing where she was given the responsibility of ensuring the academic success of minority nursing students. She served as a part-time instructor in Education at Buffalo State College and Erie Community College. She also held the position of Supervising Teacher at the Community Action Organization of Erie County, Inc. (CAO) Head Start for a number of years. Finally, she served as a certified School Social Worker with the Buffalo Board of Education until her retirement in 1988.

Clyde Murphy has been actively involved in the community throughout her life. She served on numerous boards including Child and Adolescent Psychiatric Clinic, Erie County Mental Health Association, YWCA, United Way, the Urban League and the NAACP ACT-SO. She has volunteered with the American Red Cross, served on the United Way allocation and admission committees, been chairperson of the Urban League scholarship committee and served as general chairperson of the Western New York United Negro College Fund (UNCF). She is presently volunteering with the Council of Churches Food Pantry, Children's Defense Fund Interfaith Sabbath, Western New York Crop Walk and the Buffalo Chapter of Girl Friends, Inc. School #17 Project. She was a previous member of Jack and Jill of America, Inc., Alpha Kappa Alpha Sorority, Inc.; Women's Auxiliary of the Medical Alliance, League of Women Voters and the American Association of University Women. She was a charter member of the Buffalo Chapter of Girl Friends, Inc. and has served as its president and Conclave co-chairperson. Clyde is an avid bridge enthusiast and plays bridge and duplicate bridge with several groups. In addition, she has present and past interests in music, art, golf, reading and gardening.

Mrs. Murphy was raised in the African Methodist Episcopal tradition in Milledgeville, Georgia. In Buffalo, she has been an active member of Lincoln Memorial United Methodist Church since 1947. As a church member she has been President of the United Methodist Women, and served on the trustee board and finance committee.
Presently, she is serving on the Buffalo District United Methodist Women Project committee and the Lincoln United Methodist Church Out-Reach committee.

Her awards include the following: Buffalo Urban League Volunteer Award; UNCF Appreciation Award; Community service Award of the Year from the Black Educators Association of Western New York; Jack and Jill of America, Inc., Award for Guidance and Direction; UNCF Meritorious Service Award and a Certificate of Appreciation from the Task Force Head Start.

Ophelia Nicholas

Ophelia A. Nicholas, retired educator, was the first African American female to become a principal in the Buffalo Public School system in 1969. There she served for over 31 years, 23 years as a principal, three years as assistant principal, and three years as a teacher. Mrs. Nicholas received both her baccalaureate and master's degrees from the University at Buffalo (UB) and also serves on the Board of Directors of the Alumni Association at UB.

Over the years, Mrs. Nicholas has received numerous educational, public service and appreciation awards for her life accomplishments. Some of those include the Heritage of Caring Award, an award of appreciation from the Buffalo Area Council of Churches; Phi Beta Sigma Theta Sorority, Inc. Greater Buffalo Red Cross' Outstanding Service Awards, and others.

Mrs. Nicholas is an active member of Lincoln Memorial United Methodist Church and was former board member of the Beechwood Continuing Care over 18 years. Moreover, she has been an active member of the Delta Sigma Theta Sorority, Inc. for over 44 years where she served as past president of the Gamma Kappa Chapter from 1961-1962.

Frances Taliaferro Price

Frances Taliaferro Price is a retired educator who attended Buffalo State Teachers College where she received her Bachelors, Masters and Superintendent's Certificate. Later, she graduated from Erie Technical Institute and worked in the Food Service and Dietary Department of General Hospital.

She is very active in her church, First Shiloh Baptist, where she served over ten years as the President of the Deaconess Board. She has enriched her church's program through her spiritual leadership and talents heading the church's oldest auxiliary - the Willing Workers Club, which sponsors the "Harvest Celebration of Talent." Each year this program enables untapped talent to surface and also raises funds to enhance the function and beauty of God's House.

Mrs. Price is an active member of the community. She was President of the Women's Auxiliary of the NAACP and has been a life member for over ten years. Mrs. Price is a member of many community organizations and has received numerous awards and recognition for her creativity and unselfish sharing.

She is known as "A World Traveler." She and her husband traveled extensively during their time of employment and continued during their retirement. Some of the places visited include most of the U.S.A., Alaska and Hawaii, many of the warm islands including Puerto Rico, South America and Mexico. They traveled to Paris, London, and Amsterdam, "Home" to Senegal, Africa and later to Hong Kong, Bangkok, Bali, Rome, Singapore, Madrid and Barcelona. And they are still planning to visit other places. These experiences are always shared with friends and relatives with many interesting presentations of slides and pictures.

Mrs. Price is married to Judson Price. They have three daughters; Judine D. Agnostini, Sandra L. Allen, and Monica J. Price - all are graduates of Buffalo State College. They have five grandchildren: Desmond J. Allen, Alliah D. Agostini, Lamar Allen, Alana Agostini, and Reginald Allen.

Josephine Hunter Robbins

Josephine Hunter Robbins was born and raised in Raleigh, North Carolina. Josephine completed her formative education in her home city. She completed studies for a Bachelor of Science degree in biology at Bennett College in Greensboro, North Carolina. After moving to Buffalo, she earned both her Masters in Secondary Education as well as the Certification in Administration and Supervision from Buffalo State College.

Mrs. Robbins began her career in 1956 as a science teacher. From 1956 to 1959, she taught in two public schools in Raleigh. She re-located to Buffalo, New York in 1960. Her teaching career in the Buffalo Public Schools spanned a 35 year period and included six years teaching junior high school science and ten years as an Administrator, with teaching assignments in science, chemistry and biology. This latter position was at St. Augustine's School/Fulton Academic Complex, a school for pregnant and parenting teens. Mrs. Robbins concluded her teaching career as the secondary principal at St. Augustine's/Fulton Academic Complex. She retired in 1995.

She has been a member of St. Philip's Episcopal Church since 1989. She has served numerous terms on the Vestry, including serving as Warden of the Parish. She has also served as the Superintendent of the Sunday school. She actively serves as a Lay Eucharistic Minister of the Parish. At the Diocesan level, she has served on the Diocesan Council, Episcopal Church Home Board, Board of Episcopal Community Services, Board of Ventures in Faith, Lay Episcopal Youth Council Advisor of the Central Erie Deanery, Urban Missioner Committee and Diocesan Commission on Ministries.

Her community involvement reflects the high level of her commitment to community service. Past community participation includes membership on the Infant Mortality Task Force, Erie County Health Advisory Board, National Youth Sports Program Advisory Committee, Erie County EEO Hearing Complaint Board, National Association Concerned with School Age Parents, Governor's Task Force on Teen Pregnancy, Buffalo Teachers' Federation, Buffalo Secondary Principals' Association, National Association for

Secondary School Principals, National Association for Supervision and Curriculum Development, Black Educators' Association, Western New York Coalition on Teen Pregnancy, St. Augustine's Community Center Board of Directors, Deaconess Hospital Family Planning Advisory Board, March of Dimes Advisory Board, and Board of Directors of Homespace, Inc.

Mrs. Robbins is also an active member of Alpha Kappa Alpha Sorority, Inc., Gamma Phi Omega Chapter. She serves on the St. Philip's Community Center Board and volunteers for Women for Human Rights and Dignity.

She has received a number of awards including, Community Service Award and the Angels for Service Award from Women for Human Rights and Dignity; Outstanding Community Service in Education Award; Humanitarian and Caring Award, Alpha Kappa Alpha Sorority, Inc., Great Lakes Region and Woman of the Year Award from Zeta Phi Beta Sorority.

Mrs. Robbins was married to the late James Edward Robbins. She has two stepchildren and five step grandchildren.

Genevieve Stevenson Stenhouse

Genevieve Stenhouse, more affectionately known at "Gen," is the second of four children to Lofton and Robertha Stevenson. Her parents hailed from South Carolina, however, she was born and raised in Buffalo, New York. She was educated in Buffalo Public Schools, and attended Buffalo State Teacher's College where she earned a Bachelor of Arts degree in Elementary Education in 1974, a Masters of Education degree in Reading in 1976, and an Elementary and Reading certification also in 1976.

A member of Pleasant Grove Missionary Baptist Church for over 50 years, Genevieve has held several lay and ministerial leadership roles. As a faithful member of the Senior Choir, she has held the offices of President, Secretary and Treasurer. She has also been Directress of the Board of Christian Education for most of her membership at Pleasant Grove. In 1995, the pastor asked Genevieve to institute Saturday Bible classes for individuals aged five through adulthood. The classes, which run September through May, have been instrumental in helping Pleasant Grove members to embrace and live the word of God not only on Sundays, but through their daily lives.

Genevieve and Thomas, her husband of over fifty years, met as youngsters when they lived in the downtown section of Buffalo, and attended the same neighborhood elementary school and church. They married at an early age. Thomas worked two jobs while attending college to provide a good quality of life for his family. Genevieve supported her husband's efforts by maintaining their home, working part-time jobs while the children were in school and carefully developing and maintaining the household budget. Her faith in God and country led her to begin buying United States Savings Bonds early in their marriage for the family's education. Their consistent, payday additions to this nest egg helped them fund their children's and Genevieve's baccalaureate education programs, without the need for student loans.

Genevieve currently resides in Buffalo with her husband of 54 years, Thomas Henry Stenhouse. She is the mother of Robert Lee Stenhouse (Phyllis), Dr. Thomasina Rochelle Stenhouse, and "son-in-love" Dennis Dixon. She has numerous grandchildren including Derek Lewis Stenhouse (Yolanda), Shannon Rochelle Stenhouse and Robert Devin Stenhouse; and she is the great-grandmother of Ebone Danielle Buggs, Maxine Rachel-Rochelle Stenhouse, Miles Thomas Stenhouse, and Makenzy Noel Yvonne Stenhouse. Genevieve is proud of the fact that her children and grandchildren are all college graduates. Together the family has earned twelve post-secondary degrees, plus one professional certification. Formal education, achievement and service are values that have been passed down from generation to generation in the Stenhouse family.

In addition to her role as Directress of the Board of Christian Education at Pleasant Grove Missionary Baptist Church, Genevieve served over fifteen years as a reading specialist and elementary teacher in the Buffalo Public School System. She referred to her charges as "darlings" and they knew they were her beloveds. I Thessalonians 5:11 says “Therefore encourage one another and build each other up.” Encourager is a term that characterizes Genevieve's relationship with her students. "Go ahead, you can do it!" was the mantra in her classroom.

Genevieve's favorite saying is: If you make one step, God will make two. Her favorite scripture is Psalm 121. Armed with her faith in God's word, she has weathered several of life's storms valiantly, with seemingly increasing strength, and to the benefit of all who know her.

Lillie P.W. Stevens

The first African American female to graduate from the private University at Buffalo with a degree in Physical Education, Lillie also attended Bethune-Cookman College. She later earned her master's degree in education from the University at Buffalo and became the first Black Physical Education teacher and first Black female administrator in the Niagara Falls School District. She was later elected as the President of the 100,000 plus member University at Buffalo Alumni Association.

Her professional career began more than forty-five years ago with service in the Buffalo, Williamsville, and Niagara Falls School Districts that included receipt of tenure in four areas.

Mrs. Stephens is affiliated with four Prince Hall Masonic organizations, having served as President of two of them. After serving as teacher for fifteen years and an administrator for twenty-two, her last five years of employment were spent in the role of Principal at 60th Street Elementary School in Niagara Falls, New York. She remains active on several Boards of Directors, both locally and nationally.

In addition to her vast career in the field of education, Lillie has received numerous honors and awards due to her involvement in the aforementioned communities. Some of her many awards include: WHLD and Tops Markets Top Hat Award, Magnet Schools of America Award for National Service and Dedication, National Association of Education Equity Award for twenty-two years of Service; Niagara Falls Black Achievers Association Lifetime

Achievement Award, Black Educators' Association of Western New York Educator of the Year Award, Coalition of 100 Black Women Buffalo Chapter Spotlight on Women Award; *Who's Who Among Women in the World*, Alpha Kappa Alpha Sorority, Inc., Gamma Phi Omega Chapter, Humanitarian Award, Niagara Falls Chapter of The Links Incorporated, Woman of the Month in Education Award and others.

Lillie Stephens holds active memberships in many local, regional, national and international organizations including: Alpha Kappa Alpha Sorority, Inc. (life member); Phi Delta Kappa (Academic) Fraternity, Inc.; Zonta International of Amherst; The Buffalo College Club; National Committee for School Desegregation (charter member and past president); NAACP (life member); Magnet Schools of America (board member) and Family and Children Services of Niagara County (life member).

She resides with her husband, Edward, in Williamsville. Lillie and Edward are the parents of two children and grandparents to three. They are active members of Calvary Episcopal Church.

Michelle Thomas

Mrs. Michelle J. Thomas is head of the music department at The Park School of Buffalo and Organist at Faith Baptist Church.

Michelle began studying piano in 1955 and organ in 1959. She won First Place - Piano Competition, National Eastern Star Conferences in 1961, 1962; and First Place - Piano Competition, James Cleveland Gospel Music Workshop of America in 1979. She was Assistant Director and accompanist for the St. Philip's Boys and Young Men's Choir under the direction of Donald L. Hilliard (former Supervisor of Music, Buffalo Public Schools). The Boys choir performed with the Buffalo Philharmonic Orchestra under the direction of Maestro Michael Tilson Thomas from 1980 through 1985. Later the choir was renamed Buffalo Arts and Music Youth Chorale (and girls were added), under the direction of Maestro Julius Rudel. This group was selected to represent the United States at the Tenth International Youth and

Music Festival held in Vienna, Austria in July 1981. They won awards at the National Association of Negro Musicians, Detroit Michigan, in July 1985 and performed at the MENC Conference of National Educators Association (NEA) Miami, Florida in 1985.

Michelle was a Choir Director and pianist at the University at Buffalo during the most Reverend Desmond M. Tutu's visit to Buffalo in January 1989, as well as for the Buffalo Philharmonic Orchestra's Dr. Martin Luther King Jr. Concert. Some of the music featured on that concert Michelle had performed in 1973 at Chautauqua Lake. Twenty years later she was accompanist for the Buffalo State College Singers under the direction of Dr. Raymond Tymas-Jones.

Michelle was the accompanist for the 1991 Western New York World University Games Choir in Sheffield, England. Her performances as a part of the Buffalo Philharmonic Orchestra Black History Concerts have been especially gratifying, and her duet with Doc Severinsen at the Pops Series Finale in 1996 was particularly unforgettable.

In May of 1997 she received a Certificate of Special Congressional Recognition from the House of Representatives and an Achievement Award from the City of Buffalo for a music school she started at the Faith Baptist Church. More recently (January 1997-98), she was guest organist for the New York State Dr. Martin Luther King, Jr. Holiday Memorial Observance at the State Capitol in Albany, New York. Michelle, an accomplished composer, was selected in April 1999 to assist and accompany the group New Beginnings in Dortmond, Germany during the Buffalo/Dortmond Sister City Cultural Exchange. Michelle accompanied two groups of performers for the visit of President Clinton, Vice President Gore and their families in January, 1999 in Buffalo.

The Common Council, City of Buffalo, declared Sunday, August 22, 1999, "Michelle Thomas Day" in the City of Buffalo in honor of her 40th year of music service.

Alice Holloway Young

Alice Holloway Young was born on September 29 in Warrenton, Warren County, North Carolina. She received a Bachelor of Science degree from Bennett College and Masters and Doctoral degrees in Education Supervision and Administration from the University of Rochester. She became employed with the Rochester City School District in 1952 and pioneered as an African American educator over the next four decades. A gifted teacher, an untiring advocate and administrator, she is recognized as an energetic champion for the school children of New York State and had a pronounced influence upon Rochester higher education.

In many of her achievements, Dr. Holloway was the first in the field. For example, she was one of the District's first African American Classroom teachers; the only African American reading specialist in the District; the first Vice Principal and Principal of elementary schools; first Title I Director (programs for educationally and economically deprived children; wrote and supervised the District's first integration programs including the Urban Suburban Program which is still in existence and other firsts as well.

Her list of awards include the About Time Exemplar Community Uplift Award, Urban League of Rochester's Distinguished Community Service Award, Award for Humanitarian and Distinguished Achievement in Community Service, the Civic Award from the Rochester Area Chamber of Commerce for Meritorious Contributions in the Field of Education, the University of Rochester Distinguished Alumna Award and the highest honor conferred by the State University of New York Association of the Boards of Trustees of Community Colleges, the Anne M. Bushnell Memorial Award for Special Achievement.

Dr. Young is a former fellow at R.I.T., a charter member of the Athenaeum and a former president of the five country Rochester Area Chapter of Phi Delta Kappa Fraternity, the Delta Kappa Gamma International Education Society and the Rochester Chapter of The Links, Incorporated; Warden of St. Luke and St. Simon Cyrene

Episcopal Church and active in The Episcopal Diocese of Western New York. She is a member of Delta Nu Omega Chapter of Alpha Kappa Alpha Sorority, Inc.

Dr. Young, named a trustee in 1961, helped to establish Monroe Community College. Overall, her commitment to the college has lasted more than four decades, serving as a Chair of its Trustees for twenty consecutive years (1978-1998) and recognized as the trustee who has served the college and the New York State community colleges the longest.

To help continue her mission and efforts to educate all of Rochester's children, Monroe Community College (MCC) inaugurated the Alice H. Young Teaching Internship for Ethnic Minority Graduate students in 1987. This unique program provides MCC students with a more culturally diverse faculty while giving them valuable teaching experience at a community college.

The Alice Holloway Young Society for Charitable Giving of the MCC Foundation was established to honor Dr. Young as a twentieth-century American pioneer in education.

Sandra Leah Walker

Sandra Leah Walker was born in Buffalo, New York on July 17, 1944. She is the oldest child of the late Samuel S. Walker, Sr. and Georgie Stokes Walker, both originally of Calhoun Falls, SC. Her brother, Samuel resides in California and her younger sister by almost 17 years, Sonia Lynn, resides with her in Buffalo.

She and her siblings are proud to be the third generation of five living generations. Her grandmother, Lucille Lee Stokes is 97 and was also born in Calhoun Falls, SC. She is the mother of Leah Andria Johnson (David) Behrens and Thomas William (Tiffany) Johnson Jr. and has been blessed with three grandsons, David Paul Behrens III, age 3, Gabriel Thomas Behrens, age 1, and Christian Thomas Johnson, age 1.

Sandra was graduated from P.S. #17 and Lafayette High School. She completed Buffalo State College in a three year accelerated program in Elementary Education with a minor in Spanish in the Elementary School. After briefly being employed at the New York State Employment Service, she began a career with the Buffalo Public Schools in April 1966. In 1973 she was selected by the school system and the University at Buffalo to participate in a program to train teachers to become School Counselors. She received a Masters of Education in 1974. She retired as a School Counselor at McKinley High School in June 2000.

Sandra is a 50-year member of the Lutheran Church of Our Savior. She taught Sunday School, the Adult Bible Class, and was the Administrator of the RagTime Vacation Bible School; sang in the Junior Choir, Senior Choir, and Voices of God Choir; was the Council Secretary and is Parliamentarian for the Church Council. In 1987 she was the third woman elected to the Board of Deacons and in October 2000 she became the first woman elected as Chair of the Board of Deacons.

In October 1963, Sandra became a member of Alpha Kappa Alpha Sorority, Inc. and is the immediate past president of Xi Epsilon Omega Chapter located in Amherst, New York. She is on the Board of Directors of LADD (Lutheran Association for the Developmentally Disabled) and is a member of the Task Force for Mission Development for the Lutheran Church-Missouri Synod in the city of Buffalo. She is a member of the NAACP and Urban League and has voted in every election since age 18.

Sandra, the National Foote Family Reunion Treasurer, and her sister, Sonia, the National Foote Family Reunion President renewed their interest in genealogy after attending a reunion in 1986. They are researching both Walkers and Footes. The Walker line stems from their father. The Foote line stems from their maternal great-grandmother, Leah Foote Lee who was married to David Lee, the parents of their grandmother, Lucille Lee Stokes.

While, we may never know our home tribe from Africa, we hope to leave future generations with knowledge, information, and pride in who they are.

Uncrowned Queens in Health

Ellen E. Grant Bishop

Ellen E. Grant Bishop is a Buffalo native who began her career as a nurse at Erie County Medical Center in 1968. Dr. Bishop then worked at Buffalo General Hospital for 15 years. When she left the General in 1988, she was vice president and administrator of its Community Health Center.

Dr. Bishop was the first African American to be appointed Erie County Mental Health Commissioner. She served in this position, under the administration of Erie County Executive Dennis T. Gorski, for 12 years.

In January 2001, Dr. Bishop was appointed chief executive officer of Niagara Falls Memorial Medical Center and was the first woman to hold the title of CEO since the hospital was formed in 1895. Under Dr. Bishop's leadership a Women's Health Initiative that included a refurbished OB-GYN unit and a community services center was opened. Following her position at Niagara Falls Memorial Medical Center, Dr. Bishop has worked as a consultant with clients throughout the United States.

Dr. Bishop serves on numerous boards, including St. Bonaventure University, the Western New York Healthcare Association, the Western New York Women's Fund, and the Black Women's Health Study at Boston University's School of Medicine. She is the past President of the New York State Association of Counties and the current president of the New York State Chapter Board of Directors of the National Association of Social Workers.

Dr. Bishop has received numerous awards and citations and in 1996 received an Honorary Doctorate for Exemplary Community Service from Medaille College in Buffalo.

Ina R. Chapman

Ina Rebecca Doss Chapman was born in Buffalo, New York and attended Buffalo Public Schools. She is the youngest of six siblings born to Elizabeth and the late Monroe Doss.

She has a long career in the health sciences and has several certifications from programs such as the American Society of Clinical Pathologists in Contemporary Issues in Flow Cytometry, the Beckman/Dickinson Immunocytometry Systems, Basic Radiation Safety from the University at Buffalo and the Baylor College of Medicine in Health Education. Believing that one should have balance in their lives, she also has certification as a fitness instructor and lifeguard.

For twenty years, Inca worked at Roswell Park Cancer Institute as a Medical Research Technician in Flow Cytometry, Radiation Medicine, and Cancer Control and Epidemiology. In 2002, she was appointed Executive Outreach Coordinator for the Witness Project of Buffalo and Erie County. This is a national cancer education replication and dissemination project, originating at the University of Arkansas at Little Rock. The Buffalo and Erie County project is one of thirty-two sites across the country. The primary goal of the project is to educate the African American community about breast and cervical cancer as well as emphasizing the importance of early detection.

As coordinator, she works with a dedicated team of over thirty staff and volunteers and is responsible for supervising training, conducting seminars and workshops for other organizations, and recruiting lay health advisors and Witness role models. She also works with members of the community through businesses, churches, and community centers to teach women about breast self-exams and cervical cancer screening. Ina Chapman is a member of the Roswell Park Alliance Annual Fund Committee and is a much sought after public speaker.

In 2003, she began a new role as the first lady of the St. John Baptist Church and succeeds in managing a delicate balance between work and church.

She shares a twenty-eight year commitment with her husband, Rev. Michael Chapman. They are residents of the City of Buffalo and are the proud parents of five children, Kenyatta Jameel, Mikeyta Irene, Tiffany Oria, Tera Elizabeth, Michael II, and 14 grandchildren.

Virginia Daniels Chavers

Virginia Daniels Chavers is a former professional model. She is also a registered nurse with a Bachelor's Degree in Nursing, and an Associate's Degree in Applied Science. She completed graduate work in Vocational Education at Buffalo State College. Virginia also has a license as a Real Estate salesperson.

She spent her formative years in Chicago where she was born and has three sisters and ten half sisters and brothers. She gives honor to her mother, who has been a great influence in her life.

Virginia received her initial training in the Cook County Hospital in Chicago. Soon after completing her training, she moved to Buffalo with her mother and started work at the Buffalo General Hospital. She was soon given Charge Nurse responsibilities and at times was in charge of three units on one shift.

Friends and acquaintances often asked Virginia if she had ever thought of modeling. At their urging, she decided to get some training and give modeling a try. She enrolled in the prestigious Ferrel School of Charm and Modeling. Later, she enrolled in June II, the best agency available in the area. Owner and model June Visserhoff was her agent. Modeling became a segue into an exciting and rewarding career in every way.

Virginia's style can be described in one word, panache (gentle elegance). She became a popular choice of the fashion coordinators and photographers around the Buffalo area. She was usually the only African American model in a show and her modeling jobs were financially rewarding.

She was a frequent model for Adam, Meldrum and Anderson Department Store's runway shows and Tea Room Specialty shows. There were also beautiful shows for Tegler's and extravagant and lavish fundraiser shows at Wm. Hengerer's. In addition she made regular appearances on the television shows *Dialing for Dollars* and *T.V. Auctions*. Occasionally, her children's teachers would allow them and their classmates to watch Virginia on these television programs. She also modeled for Slotkins, Mable Danahy and many others.

Virginia was also a photographers' model. She worked with several well-known photographers including Sherwin Greenberg Studios, Hobart Studios and the Lensmeister Studio. After the hospital and modeling experience, Virginia went on to other accomplishments and returned to nursing.

She became the first Head Nurse on a supervisory level in an Erie County Health Department Center. She also worked in the Jesse Nash Center for ten years. While there, she also sold high-end real estate for the Amherst office of Stovroff and Herman, acquiring thirteen pieces of property of her own in the interim. Her advice to the women of today is "to never limit yourself, and not to let anyone else limit you!"

Virginia is involved in a number of community and civic groups including the Linwood Church of Christ, the National Association of Negro Business and Professional Women's Clubs, Inc. where she holds the offices of Secretary, Theater Chair, and Political Education Chair; the NAACP and a former member of the Gloria J. Parks Community Center. She received the Community Service Award from that organization and a Gold Card service award from the African American Cultural Center. Virginia has a number of hobbies and interests including drawing and art projects, the theater, health teaching and reading good books. She has a son Douglas II, and two daughters, Brenda and Crystill.

Zola Crowell

Zola Crowell is a native of Andalusia, Alabama. Her parents, the late Lester and Lurine Cauley Lowery, moved the family to Niagara Falls, New York in the early 1950s. Zola has over thirty years of work experience with the Federal Government including the Veterans Medical Center and the United States Postal Service. A graduate of the Niagara Falls Public School system, she attended the University at Buffalo's Millard Fillmore College and the Empire State College.

Zola has a long record of community service for which she has received numerous awards and recognitions. Her awards include: Special Contributions Award, the Veterans Medical Center; Community Service Award, The Links, Incorporated; Services to the Youth of Niagara Falls Award, The Links, Incorporated; Frontier Chapter American Business Women and the New York Historical Awareness Award from the United States Postal Service.

Writing poetry and genealogy are among the activities of which Zola is most proud. One of her poems, "Childhood Memories," was presented to former First Lady, and current New York State Senator, Hillary Rodham Clinton. Genealogy has also been a favorite pastime and has led to the discovery of a great-great-grandmother named Charity Butler. Charity was born into slavery on the Butler plantation and lived to be 106 years of age.

Zola is actively involved in several professional and civic organizations including: The Niagara Falls Chapter of The Links, Incorporated; the Association of Black Social Workers; the Harriet Tubman 300's; the Black Pioneers of the Niagara Frontier and the American Business Women's Association. She is a member of the First Shiloh Baptist Church, a former member of the choir, the Willing Workers and The Mother's Club. Zola is also the proud mother of one daughter, Ingrid, a graduate of Johnson C. Smith University located in Charlotte, North Carolina.

Gladys Jean Diji

Gladys Jean Diji began her career as a Licensed Practical Nurse in 1973. She earned a Bachelor of Science Degree in Nursing from D'Youville College in 1986 and a Master of Science in Nursing from D'Youville in 1991. Gladys also earned another specialty in Community Addictions Nursing from D'Youville in 1998 and was asked to join the faculty in 1998.

Gladys also is employed by the Buffalo Psychiatric Center for the New York State Office of Mental Health. For over twenty-four years, she has worked in different capacities at the facility including Licensed Practical Nurse, RN staff nurse, Supervising Nurse, and Community Mental Health Nurse Program Manager. Her most recent accomplishment at the facility is her appointment to Acting Diversity Planning and Compliance Administrator.

Gladys holds a few special interests dear to her. She is specifically interested in the impact of prayer and spiritual care on health, the focus of her research project in graduate school. She is also interested in the impact of culture on health related illnesses and improving health care education.

She has a history of community involvement and has been the recipient of several awards and honors including the Quality Assurance Award from Buffalo Psychiatric Center, for which she is a three-time recipient, and the Award of Appreciation from the Buffalo Public Schools. Gladys maintains her commitment to caring for the needs of others through her involvement in the church community. She is a parish nurse at the St. John Baptist Church and was appointed by the Pastor to serve on the committee to develop an eight-bed, faith-based hospice and palliative care facility in the Buffalo Fruitbelt Community.

Gladys serves on the Board of Directors of the Buffalo Federation of Neighborhood Centers, Inc. (BFNC), a human service organization providing services to individuals with mental and developmental disabilities. She also serves on committees at D'Youville College such as the Health and Wellness Committee, Education Committee, and she chairs the Diversity Planning and Compliance Advisory Committee. She is also a member of several service organizations including Alpha Kappa Alpha Sorority, Inc., Gamma Phi Omega Chapter and the Sigma Theta Tau International Nursing Honor Society, Zeta Nu Chapter.

Her hobbies include dancing and travel. Known in her childhood as an excellent dancer, Gladys won the many dancing and hula-hoop contests held at the municipal housing street dances where she lived as a child.

Gladys has three daughters: Renee, Lisa, and Tameka, eight grandchildren, and one great-grandson. She is married to Augustine and additions to the family are a stepson, Augustine, Jr., stepdaughter Angela, and granddaughter. Gladys says being the mother of five children, nine grandchildren, and one great-grandchild adds greater blessings to her life.

Bertha M. Bradley Hill

Ms. Bertha M. Bradley Hill has dedicated her entire life to health and health related issues in the Black community in Buffalo, New York. She was born in Buffalo on July 20, 1932. Although she describes herself as being born "with a physical handicap, a woman, Black, and poor," and characterizes her struggle as "knocking, kicking, slamming, shouting, begging, fighting, screaming, crying, pushing, and shoving to tear down the walls of discrimination in America," she epitomizes the essence of professional and personal community service.

Bertha Hill began her career in 1952 at the Millard Fillmore Hospital as a "helper," but was soon promoted to "nursing assistant" due to her "can-do attitude." She briefly left Buffalo to go to school in Chicago, Illinois where she received a certificate in License Practical Nursing (L.P.N.) from Greiger Vocational School in 1961. Returning to Buffalo, she received her Business Diploma from the Kensington Business School in Buffalo in 1968. She received a diploma from Edward J. Meyer Memorial Hospital in Registered Nursing and a Bachelor of Science Nursing Degree from Daeman College while married, raising a family, working in her profession, and serving her church and surrounding community.

At the age of 66, she graduated from Medaille College with a Bachelor of Science Degree in Health and Human Services with a grade point average of 3.9. She also received a certificate in Disability Studies. In 1981, she became the third Black professional nurse to be promoted to the Nursing Supervisor position at Roswell Park Memorial Institute, now Roswell Park Cancer Institute. In 1987, she became the second Black professional nurse to become the Director of Nursing at Sheehan Memorial Hospital. Four years later, she became the first Black Director for the Certified Nursing Assistants Program at Seventy Eight Restoration, Inc.

Today in retirement, Bertha Hill is an educator having lectured on various health-related subjects at the University at Buffalo and Educational Opportunity Center. She is a community activist and organizer on issues surrounding healthcare in the Black community and currently serves as the president for the affiliated chapter of the Sisters Network, Inc., a member of the faith-based Mind, Body, and Soul Project; the Witness Project of Buffalo and the American Cancer Society. She was founder and president of Ordered Steps, a human service community organization; People Assisting People Outreach Ministry (P.A.P.), a faith-based program at Grace Tabernacle Church of God and Christ where she is a member and part of the initial group who worked with her late Pastor Elder Houston Williams, to spearhead the founding of the Grace Manor Nursing Home. This nursing home is the first and only Western New York African American nursing home. She served on its Board of Directors from 1983-2000 and continues to volunteer when needed.

She has received numerous awards including: Certificate of Appreciation and Outstanding Service Citation in Nursing Service from Roswell Park Memorial Institute, the Edward J. Meyer School of Nursing Alumni Association Award, the American Cancer Society title Voice of Hope in Erie County, Distinguished Service Award from the Community Interaction Committee at Sheehan Memorial Hospital and the Nurse of Distinction Award for her commitment to the Nursing Profession from the Buffalo Metropolitan Black Nurses Association.

Claudia Lee

Claudia Lee is a native Buffalonian. She began her career in health as a Licensed Practical Nurse in 1964 after graduating from the former Fosdick Masten Vocational High School. Since then she has received her Bachelor of Science degree in nursing and Master's degree in health systems from the University at Buffalo.

Ms. Lee has a wide background in the health field and has served in many capacities. In addition to working in area hospitals and community health centers, she taught nursing at the E.J. Meyer Memorial Hospital School of Nursing and was instrumental in the development of the first minority recruitment program at the SUNY School of Nursing.

In 1983, she began her career as a Community Health Nurse Consultant at the New York State Department of Health. In 1987, she moved to Albany where she became Assistant Coordinator of the Family Planning Program for the Bureau of Reproductive Health. She joined the AIDS Institute in 1990 where she managed the HIV/AIDS Prison Program until 1993. At that time she became Bureau Director for the Bureau of Community Based Services. In 1996, she was appointed Director of the Local Health Services Unit and was responsible for the administration and management of more than $150 million in state aid to county health departments statewide. Her most recent position in Albany was as Acting Director of the Bureau of Child and Adolescent Health Services. Currently, she is the Assistant Regional Administrator for the New York State Department of Health, Western Regional Office located in Buffalo.

While in Albany, Ms. Lee was involved in numerous community and volunteer activities. She served on the United Way Allocations Committee, the Urban League Guild, the National Forum for Black Public Administrators the Albany Chapter of the Black Nurses Association and the Governor's Committee for the Annual Martin Luther King Day Celebration. Since returning to Buffalo, she has become actively involved in her church and continues to serve on community boards and projects.

She is the recipient of the 1988 Black Achiever's Recognition Award, numerous New York State Department of Health Commissioner Recognition Awards, and the United Way of Albany Volunteer Award. More recently, Ms. Lee received a recognition award from a Buffalo-based CBO for her ten years of support and advocacy for HIV/AIDS Programs in the community.

She is the mother of one son and the proud grandmother of four grandchildren.

Veronica Mason

Veronica Mason is the fourth of nine children born to Bobby and Connie Jones. She is a native of Niagara Falls, New York. Veronica states that she has overcome many obstacles as a result of her faith and her drive to succeed as a health care professional. She is a graduate of Erie County Community College where she received an Associate's degree. She received her Bachelor's degree from Daeman College. She is a Family Nurse Practitioner with a nursing degree from D'Youville College. She plans to enroll in a doctoral program at the University at Buffalo.

Veronica has been an active community volunteer serving on the Center for Young Children and Mental Health Association boards in Niagara County. She has also taught at Trocaire College and Orleans Niagara BOCES. While she was unsuccessful in starting a local chapter of the Black Nurses Association in Niagara County, she plans to resume efforts to create the chapter. She is currently a member of Living Word Church in Niagara Falls and serves as the church's special events coordinator. She is also actively engaged in outreach to other churches in the Falls area. As a nurse practitioner with a specialty in pain management, Veronica would like to eventually establish a pain management clinic in Niagara Falls.

Veronica is married to Myron Mason and has three children, Mahogany, Kelvonia, and Vanessa. Veronica states that her "vision for the future is to start a mentorship program in Niagara Falls where

I can help African Americans achieve their dreams in education, as education is the way out of poverty."

Parmalier Dejoie Murphy

Parmalier Dejoie Murphy was born in New Orleans, Louisiana. Her father was Paul H.V. Dejoie, Jr., an insurance executive and founder of the Unity Insurance Company, one of the first African American insurance companies in the south. Her mother was Thelma Epps Dejoie, proprietor and designer of Dejoie's Floral Shoppee. Parmalier has two sisters, Paulette Hamlet of Washington, D.C. and Ellie Jenkins of Vineyard Haven, Massachusetts.

Parmalier attended Xavier University of New Orleans, Louisiana and obtained a Bachelor of Science degree. She was a member of the college choir, the Xavier Solidarity Club and Alpha Kappa Alpha Sorority, Inc. She was awarded a special New Orleans Teacher's Certification. In the community, Parmalier became a charter member of the Black Junior League, a service organization that responded to area needs.

Parmalier also attended Meharry Medical College and obtained certification as a Medical Technologist (A.S.C.P.) and was employed by Meharry Medical College as a clinical instructor, medical technologist and research technologist. She is the author of two articles: "Detection of Lupus Erythematosis Cells" (1950), *and* "Eosinophil Counts in Pre and Post Operative Surgery" (1951), both in the American Medical Association Journal. After her relocation to Buffalo, New York, she was a supervisor of Paraprofessional Programs of the University at Buffalo Urban Center. Other Buffalo work experiences include directorship of the Buffalo Negro Scholarship Foundation and working as a science teacher for the Buffalo Board of Education.

Parmalier came to Buffalo as the bride of the late Dr. Lawrence Murphy Sr. and is the mother of five and grandmother of nine. Her greatest accomplishment is the education of her children: Lawrence

Murphy Jr., Parmalier Murphy, D.D.S., Paul, Marie Murphy, Esq., and Paulette Murphy.

Parmalier has been a volunteer for the American Red Cross, Legion of Mary and Meals on Wheels. Other past affiliations include: Jack and Jill of America, Inc.; Delta Kappa Gamma Society International - Pi State; Legion of Mary, Bishop's Committee; Our Ladies Sodality; Inner City Council of Churches, Coast Guard Auxiliary - Flotilla 3-5; Alpha Kappa Alpha Sorority, Inc.; Neuman Guild; Consortium of Allied Health and Toby's Gardeners.

Her hobbies include Bridge, reading and floral design, a skill learned from her mother, a professional florist and businesswoman.

Her record of community organizations is extensive and she is active in the American Bridge Association, the American Contract Bridge League, Salvation Army, Girl Friends, Inc., The College Club of Buffalo, NAACP, St. John the Baptist Roman Catholic Church, Albright-Knox Art Gallery, Women's Dental Guild, Women Dental Bowling League, O'Hara School of Ikebana - Buffalo Chapter, Retired Teacher's Association, Inc., and the Buffalo Retired Teacher's Association.

She is the recipient of numerous awards including the Search and Rescue Award and the Emergency Communication Award from the Coast Guard Auxiliary, Appreciation Award as the Editor Coast Guard Newspaper, Local Bridge Tournaments trophies and Master Point credit awards, and a Certified Life Member of the American Bridge Association.

Parmalier states: "My hope for the future is that my family will grow in love of the Lord as we grow together through the years."

Placid J. Parker

Placid Jean Parker was born in Perth Amboy, New Jersey, where she completed her elementary and secondary education. In 1946, she earned a Diploma in Nursing from the Provident Hospital School of Nursing, located in Baltimore, Maryland. The following year, she moved to Buffalo, New York to take a position at Millard Fillmore Hospital. Mrs. Parker was a pioneer in Buffalo's health care community and was one of the first Black nurses to work at Millard Fillmore Hospital.

In 1956, Mrs. Parker joined the staff of Children's Hospital, where she was appointed as the Nursing Supervisor of the Employee's Health Office. In 1971, she received a Bachelor of Science Degree in Nursing from D'Youville College.

Subsequently, she worked for the Board of Education as the first Director of Nursing at the Fulton Street Academy. During the 1970s she was a clinical instructor and Coordinator for adult health nursing at Buffalo General Hospital School of Nursing and was in that position for more than eight years. She also founded a nursing scholarship program at Buffalo General. Later in her career, she was appointed the Director of Nursing at Sheehan Memorial Hospital. Mrs. Parker was a founder of the Practical and Registered Nursing Association.

Mrs. Parker had many interests and talents. She was an organist for the Otterbein United Methodist Church and also served as a member of the church's Board of Trustees. She was also an accomplished writer who authored several articles covering a wide range of topics including a booklet to assist in the preparation of children for hospitalization. Her paper, "The History of St. Augustine Center" can be found in the archives of The Episcopal Diocese of Western New York. She also wrote

Her many honors include the Sojourner Truth Award for outstanding community service from the Buffalo Chapter of the National Association of Negro Business and Professional Women's Clubs, as well as numerous scholastic and achievement awards from the Practical and Registered Nurses Association and the D'Youville College Alumnae Association. She was also cited in an article entitled "Middle Class Blacks" that appeared in the 1973 special edition of Ebony Magazine. In 1992, Mrs. Parker was appointed to serve on the state mental health commission by former Governor Mario Cuomo. She served on the commission until 1995. She was an active member of the Central Park United Methodist Church and served as a trustee and served on the standing committee for archives and history in Western New York.

Mrs. Parker departed this life on July 2, 1996, and is buried in Forest Lawn Cemetery.

Juanita Pitts

Dr. Juanita G. Pitts is a native of Birmingham, Alabama. She graduated from Englewood High School and Wilson Junior College of Chicago. She completed studies at Livingstone College in North Carolina with a double major, receiving a B.S. in Chemistry and Biology. She was a teaching assistant at Tuskegee Institute where she pursued a M.S. in Biochemistry and conducted studies in Dr. George Washington Carver's lab. After working as an instructor in biological sciences at Livingstone College, Dr. Pitts received a fellowship to the Department of Biochemistry at Howard University in Washington, D.C. There she worked at various job including lab instructor in neuro-anatomy, lab assistant in biochemistry, and departmental secretary for the Department of Microbiology. She completed her medical degree in 1954.

Dr. Pitts and Julian O. Carroll, M.D., who also received the medical doctorate from Howard, were married and moved to Rochester. She completed her internship and residency at Highland Hospital and later with her husband, opened a joint practice providing complete family care. Incorporating time for her practice with raising seven children, made Dr. Pitts aware of the lack of community day care for working parents. She called upon family members, friends and the community to found the Community Child

Care Center. The Center was staffed by professional and paraprofessionals and was financed by family, friends and small businesses and has been in operation for 32 years. Dr. Pitts was later awarded a Headstart grant to work among migrant children of the surrounding county.

While attending the University of Rochester to pursue a master's degree in community health, she also worked for the New York State Department of Mental Health. In subsequent years she organized and executed two projects related to community health: screening for Sickle Cell Anemia along with genetic counseling and screening for hypertension and cardiovascular risk factors. Her program, in conjunction with the American Heart Association, brought the first Mobile Health unit to the city, testing for such risk factors as cholesterol, blood sugar levels and blood pressure and providing EKGs.

She served as a consultant for three years to a Sickle Cell project on the Eastern Shore of Maryland. She also continued to make house calls, and assisted several other physicians with their private practices. She volunteered for other community concerns and performed physical examinations for the Monroe County Health Department, the Rochester City School District and was Emergency Physician for the Rochester Youth Detention Center.

The President of Livingstone College and the Dean of Howard University also asked her to conduct the local admissions interviews of Western New York for the schools. Through Rochester's Mayor's office, she became a member and was later nominated as a Trustee and served as Vice President of the Frederick Douglass Memorial and Historical Association. She has also served on the master's thesis review committee for students of Christian Education at Colgate Rochester Divinity School.

Dr. Pitts left Rochester in 1979 to continue her career with New York State at the Jane N. Adams Developmental Center in Perrysburg, New York and then at the Gowanda Psychiatric Center. She retired from service with New York State in 1984. Since then she has actively promoted the advancement of Frederick Douglass' memory and was a founder of Friends of Frederick Douglass, Inc. Her drive to name the Rochester park area between South and Mt. Hope Avenues, which marks the site of the Douglass homestead, touches his cemetery plot and includes his Bronze statue, was realized on March 16, 1993 when the area was renamed Frederick Douglass Memorial Square. Dr. Pitts was recently recognized as an official tour guide for Rochester and Auburn, New York in the book by Charles Blockson: *The Underground Railroad.*

She maintains membership in numerous organizations including: Beta Kappa Chi Honorary Scientific Society, Delta Sigma Theta Sorority, Inc.; National Medical Association; American Medical Association; Alumni Organizations of Livingstone College and Howard University; Rochester Urban League; National Council of Negro Women, and the NAAC.

Her list of awards and recognitions are numerous and include: the Empire State Federation of Colored Women's Clubs Representative Service Award; Community Service Award from Daughters of ELKS, IBPOE; National Sojourner Truth Award through Rochester Genesee Valley Business and Professional Women's Club; Certificate for contributions to the Sickle Cell Project from Easton Community Neighborhood Center; Named Mother of the Festival by P.A.C.E. (Pan African Cultural Event); Charles T. Lunsford Award for Meritorious Community Service; 1980 Outstanding Community Educator by the Sister Clara Muhammed School; Award for Excellence in Medicine by United Church Ministries; First Black woman with a Practice in Rochester Community; Delta Dear of Delta Sigma Theta Sorority, Inc. and many, many others

She was actively involved with the Christian Education Board and Youth of the A.M.E. Zion Church and established the Pitts Pre-Kindergarten Program of cultural enrichment and worked with the "Buds of Promise."

Gloria Roseboro

Colonel Roseboro is a product of the Buffalo Public Schools and graduated from D'Youville College School of Nursing in 1976. In 1984, she received a Master of Science Degree in Management and Business Administration from Troy State University, Troy, Alabama. She entered the United States Air Force in November 1978 and held many staff, supervisory and executive positions in a twenty-five year Air Force career.

Her many nursing positions include Staff Nurse, Obstetrical Unit, USAF Hospital Sheppard AFB, Texas; Nurse Manager, Labor and Delivery, USAF Hospital Lakenheath, RAF Lakenheath, England; and Chief, Nurse Recruiting Branch, 3534 USAF Recruiting Squadron, Richmond, Virginia, where her branch took national recognition for coming in at number one in the nation for nurse recruiting two years in a row. Major Roseboro became Supervisor, Maternal/Child Module; Supervisor, Primary Care Module; Infection Officer; Base Moulage Officer and Chief Nurse, Air Transportable Hospital, 58th Medical Group, Luke Air Force Base, Arizona, Regional Managed Care Coordinator (DoD/OSD(HA) Managed Care Demonstration Project) Delaware Valley Health Services System, Fort Dix, New Jersey; Commander, 7th Medical Operations Squadron; Chief Nurse Executive, 7th Medical Group, Dyess AFB, Texas; and Chief, Accreditation and Quality and Chief Nurse Executive, 89th Medical Group, Andrews Air Force Base, Maryland.

Currently, Colonel Roseboro is the Chief Nurse Executive, 56th Medical Group, Air Education and Training Command, Luke Air Force Base, Arizona. She is responsible for the coordination of nursing personnel and is a board certified Nursing Administrator.

Colonel Roseboro's awards and decorations include the Meritorious Service Medal (4th Oak Leaf Cluster), Air Force Commendation Medal (1st Oak Leaf Cluster), Air Force Achievement Medal, Air Force Outstanding Unit Ribbon (2nd Oak Leaf Cluster), Air Force Organizational Excellence Ribbon, National Defense Medal with bronze star, Humanitarian Medal; Air Force Long Tour, Overseas Ribbon; Air Force Longevity Ribbon (3rd Oak Leaf Cluster), Air Force Recruiting Ribbon and Air Force Basic Training Ribbon.

She is a member of the American Nurses Association, Sigma Theta Tau International Nursing Honor Society; American Red Cross Volunteer Nurse (Life Member) and Delta Sigma Theta Sorority, Inc. (Golden Life).

Colonel Roseboro recently served as the Commander, 99th Expeditionary Medical Operations Squadron during OPERATION Northern Watch and Enduring Freedom in Incirlik, Turkey. She has been selected to become Director, Organization Effectiveness where she will be in charge of healthcare software acquisitions for the Department of Defense.

Colonel Roseboro is the daughter of Alfred, (deceased) and Emma Killian. She has one daughter, Renee Dawson and granddaughter, Brittany of Alexandria, Virginia. She is the sister of Alfreda, Gregory (Warene) and Jerome Killian of Buffalo, New York and Alfred Killian of Denver, Colorado.

Before joining the military, she was a member of St. John Baptist Church where she still worships when visiting with family.

Uncrowned Queen Historians

Ora Anderson Curry

A native Buffalonian, Ora Louise Anderson was a fourth generation member of a family that has lived in Buffalo since 1832. She was a graduate of Hutchinson Central High School and earned both a bachelor and master's degree from the University at Buffalo.

Mrs. Curry was a woman of many talents including educator, historian, archivist and poet. She achieved many "firsts" in a long, distinguished career. She began her teaching career in 1958 as a history teacher in the Buffalo School District. She was the first African American teacher at Bennett High School and founded and served as the faculty advisor for the Interracial Researchers, an extracurricular student group. The group gained renown locally and nationally for its creative programs on the myths of prejudice. In 1969, the group performed its choreopoem Heartbeat in the general assembly at the annual conference of the National Education Association and received a standing ovation.
The following year, Mrs. Curry took a leave from the school district to become a master demonstration teacher in the State Education Department's Bureau of Social Studies. At the same time, she taught courses on African American history for the University at Buffalo's Millard Fillmore College. In 1971 Mrs. Curry became an administrative associate with the State Education Department. In this position she was responsible for the over-sight of state and federally funded programs in the Division of Education. Mrs. Curry retired in 1984.

Mrs. Curry was an active member of the community, who participated in numerous community organizations and activities. She was a life member of the NAACP, gave lectures and received numerous honors. She was knowledgeable of the pre-Civil War history of African Americans in Western New York, particularly as it related to her family. She also served as a consultant to the Buffalo Quarters Historical Society.

Mrs. Curry and her husband John were the parents of three daughters. She is the daughter of Uncrowned Queen Ora L. Anderson and the niece of Uncrowned Queen Amelia Anderson.

Mrs. Curry died on February 5, 2002 at age 81. Her children described her as "a friend of Buffalo; her family an icon of Buffalo history, and a tremendous source of local history."

W.J. "Joye" Hardiman

Dr. Joye Hardiman is a brilliant conceptualizer, an inspirational speaker, and a gifted storyteller. She is an educator, scholar, and cultural activist and is a frequent keynote speaker, a sought after conference participant and an accomplished institute designer. She is the daughter of Flash and Thelma Hardiman and the mother of Salmh Hardiman.

After attending the Undergraduate Writer's Workshop at the University of Iowa, she earned her BA from the University at Buffalo. She received her Doctorate in Applied Literary Studies and Urban Education from the Union Institute and is an alumnus of Harvard University's Management Development Program. Dr. Hardiman is currently the Executive Director of The Evergreen State College urban campus in Tacoma Washington and a member of the faculty.

She is a founding member and an International Executive Board Member of the Association for the Study of Classical African Civilizations. As a Summer Fulbright Scholar she conducted extensive field research in Egypt, India, Ghana, Kenya, the Yucatan, and Trinidad on the African contribution to world civilization using literary and popular culture analysis as her methodology.

The results of Dr. Hardiman's research on Ancient Egyptian literature and worldview has been published and referenced in both scholarly works and popular forums. She has been invited to speak on a number of topics including *Ancient Wisdoms, Contemporary Solutions; The Trials and Triumphs of Spiritual Warriorship; The Multi-faceted Role of Women of African Descent from Ancient to Contemporary Times; and You Can't Kill the Culture, Dialogues in the African Creative Continuum* by a variety of national and international academic, community, civic and fraternal audiences. She has also served as a consultant to the Tacoma Art Museum and the Seattle Art Museum. Dr. Hardiman has been an active member in Washington State's Higher Education institutional, curriculum and pedagogical reform efforts. She was a core facilitator and faculty for the Washington Center for Improvement in Undergraduate Education's Community College Minority Student Success Project, Ford Foundation Cultural Pluralism Summer Institut, and the FIPSE National Learning Communities Dissemination Institute.

She has worked both regionally and nationally with boards, districts, colleges, administrators, faculty, students, and staffs in numerous areas of professional development.

Brenda Moore

Dr. Brenda Moore is an Associate Professor of Sociology at the University at Buffalo, receiving her Ph.D. in Sociology from the University of Chicago. A native of Long Island, New York, and former member of the United States Army, Dr. Moore is now a prominent Military Sociologist with research interests in race and ethnic relations, gender studies, and social stratification.

Dr. Moore has numerous publications, including several journal articles and a book entitled, *To Serve My Country, To Serve My Race: The Story of the Only African American Wacs Stationed Overseas During World War II.* She has completed research for a forthcoming book, entitled Serving Our Country: *Japanese American Women in the Military During World War II.* Dr. Moore enjoys a wide range of scholarly interests, and served as a contributor to the edited book, *African Americans and the Rise of the Post Industrial City*, writing a chapter on the class status of Blacks in Buffalo.

Dr. Moore has presented dozens of conference papers, served on a number of international, national, local community, and university committees, including the 1999 White House Initiative for One America sponsored by the University at Buffalo's College of Arts and

Sciences. Serving as the organizer and host for the event, Dr. Moore brought together concerned scholars, community leaders, students, and residents of Buffalo to talk about race and ethnic issues.

A model for the university's mission of research, teaching, and service, Dr. Moore enjoys an impressive list of professional affiliations including memberships in the American Sociological Association, the Association of Black Sociologists, Toastmasters International, Board of Directors of the Inter University Seminar on Armed Forces and Society, Fordham University Press, Second World War Series Editorial Board, Associate Editor of "Armed Forces and Society: An Interdisciplinary Journal," and a member of the Women's Army Corps Veterans Association.

Joanne T. Sadler

Dr. Joanne T. Sadler is a native of Buffalo, New York where she attended Martin Luther Christian School and Lafayette High School. She attended Virginia Union University for two years before returning to Buffalo where she earned her Bachelor's degree in Education Administration from the University at Buffalo. Dr. Sadler was a Supervisor of Curriculum for the Buffalo Public Schools where she supervised the selection of textbooks and curriculum development.

For more than sixteen years, she directed the African and African American Curriculum Infusion Program. This is a program which was designed to encourage the teaching of African and African American content in all subject areas and grade levels. In her tenure as supervisor, Dr. Sadler developed and conducted numerous professional development/teaching sessions with many teachers in the Buffalo Schools. She formed a group of teachers to assist her in these activities so that the program could be expanded.

Dr. Sadler has presented seminars at Buffalo State College, the University at Buffalo, and Canisius College and has presented lectures at both state and local educational conferences and for parent and community groups in the Buffalo area. She has also been a guest on various radio programs. She retired from the Buffalo Schools in

June 2002. She is a former adjunct professor at Niagara County Community College where she taught African American History. She currently teaches at Daemen College and volunteers with the Program Committee for the Northeast YMCA.

Dr. Sadler is the author of an African American history book entitled, *Here and There, Then and Now: A History of Africans in America.* She is a member of Alpha Kappa Alpha Sorority, Inc., Gamma Phi Omega Chapter. Dr. Sadler is also the mother of two children and grandmother of one child.

Uncrowned Queens in the Media

Frances Murphy

Frances L. Murphy II, Washington publisher emeritus and editorial page editor of the *Afro-American* Newspapers, was an associate professor and head of the journalism sequence at the State University at Buffalo from 1975 to 1984. She is the sister of Carlita Murphy Jones of Buffalo and sister-in-law of the Rev. Leeland Jones, former Buffalo city councilman.

Ms. Murphy was married to the late Charles Campbell, a material control analyst for General Mills, one of the company's few Black supervisors at the time.

When Ms. Murphy first came to Buffalo she was hired as a lecturer at Buffalo State for their new Journalism Sequence, a department staffed by mostly English professors who had little or no journalism experience. She eventually was granted tenure and then given leave to do research. On her retirement from Buffalo State College, she was granted Emeritus status. Ms. Murphy had taught at Morgan State University and had been chairman of the board of the *Afro-American* Newspapers. At the Afro she had come up through the ranks at this newspaper which was founded by her grandfather John H. Murphy Sr. in 1892.

During the summer, Ms. Murphy conducted Urban Journalism Workshops for minority high school students, which started in 1978 with a grant of $3,369 from the Newspaper Fund, Inc. and an additional grant from the *Buffalo Evening News*. The purpose was to give minority journalists a realistic picture of professional journalism by having them write, publish, and edit their own newspaper.

An article by Frances Murphy written in 1977, stated that when she attended a convention of the Association for Education in Journalism, she was greatly encouraged by Thomas Engelman, executive director of the Newspaper Fund, Inc., to apply for a grant to conduct a workshop in journalism to encourage minorities to become involved in news writing.

She then wrote a proposal and took it to the managing editor of the *Buffalo Evening News* and arrangements were made for the News to give Ms. Murphy a matching grant. The proposal was later approved by the Newspaper Fund board along with 14 other grants throughout the country.

Ms. Murphy recruited high school students from the metropolitan area who then were invited to live on campus for two weeks, where they were fully saturated with how newspapers worked. Then they did stories for their own workshop newspaper. At the end of the two weeks, *The Buffalo News* published the newspaper and inserted it into its own daily newspaper.

In later years, the *News* hired some of the students who had come through the workshop and who had graduated from Buffalo State College in the journalism school. Ms. Murphy was also the advisor to the student chapter of the Society of Professional Journalists Sigma Delta Chi and received the highest award from the organization–"The Frankie Award"-- for her nickname, Frankie. For a couple of summers in order to enhance her editing skills Ms. Murphy worked on the copy desk of the Buffalo Evening News and sat in on executive editorial meetings with the opportunity for input.

While in Buffalo Ms. Murphy was an active member of the Buffalo Branch of the NAACP and served on the branch's board of directors, worked with ACT-SO and was elected to the National Board of Directors. She also served on the Board of Trustees of the NAACP Special Contribution Fund. She was also a member of St. Philip's Episcopal Church where she served on the search committee to secure a new pastor who later became a bishop.

She is a life member of Delta Sigma Theta Sorority, Inc., an organization of which her mother, Vashti Turley Murphy, was a co-founder. She is also a member of The Links, Incorporated.

A graduate of the University of Wisconsin School of Journalism, Ms. Murphy earned a B.S. degree in education from Coppin State College and an M.Ed. degree from the Johns Hopkins University. She also studied at the University of Southampton, England.

Since leaving Buffalo she has taught journalism at Howard University (1984 to 1991) and been publisher of the Washington Afro-American Newspaper. She is now publisher emeritus of the Washington Afro and editor of the editorial page of both the Washington and Baltimore Afro-American Newspapers.

In D.C., she is a past president of the Episcopal Church Women of St. Luke's Episcopal Church and past president of the Capital City

Chapter of The Links, Incorporated. She is a life member of the Washington Urban League.

Now living in the family home in Baltimore which her parents, Carl and Vashti Murphy built in 1929, Ms. Murphy is on the vestry of St. James' Episcopal Church where she sings on the Gospel Choir, is a greeter and warden (chair) of St. Agnes Guild. She is vice president of the Baltimore Chapter of The Links, Incorporated and serves on the board of directors of Stadium Place, formerly the Memorial Stadium which is now being redeveloped for homes for seniors and a YMCA. She is also listed in *Who's Who Among Black Americans, Who's Who in America* and on the History Makers website.

Her children are the Rev. Frances "Toni" Draper, pastor of John Wesley AME Zion Church in Baltimore (Andre Draper, owner of Wells Printers); Dr. James E. Wood Jr., head of orthopedic surgery at Harbor Hospital, Baltimore (Robin, Safe and Sound Inc.); Susan Murphy Wood, wife of Dr. Lance Barnes of Biloxi, Miss.; and stepsons, David Lloyd Campbell, engineer at NASA (Marlene, engineer) and Charles "Bud" Campbell, professor at Erie County Community College (Barbara, University of Buffalo). She has 17 grandchildren and four great-grandchildren with others on the way.

Uncrowned Queens in Politics and Government

Hon. Karen Ellington

Ms. Karen R. Ellington is a native of Buffalo, New York. She is one of five children, born to Marian and Willie W. Davis. Ms. Ellington is a graduate of Buffalo's Riverdale High School and the Bryant and Stratton Business Institute. Upon graduating from Bryant and Stratton Business Institute, Ms. Ellington successfully attained thirteen certificates of completion in her field of Medical Technology.

She was the First African American and the first woman elected to the Fillmore District of the City of Buffalo Common Council where her guiding principles were stewardship and service to her community and to the City of Buffalo. As former Fillmore District Council Member, Ms. Ellington had a vision for her community which began with cleaning up neighborhoods, developing a safer place for all, establishing centers and programs for seniors and children, assisting people in the community to become homeowners, encouraging business growth and promoting health, education and wellness. Ms. Ellington was very much aware of the challenges people faced daily in her community, as prior to her election, she had been a property owner for thirteen years and a Block Club President for one year in the Fillmore District.

During her term in office, Ms. Ellington served on the Educational Committee, Civil Service Committee, Finance Committee, Police Reorganization Committee, and the Broadway-Fillmore Anti-Crime Task Force of the City Council. Furthermore, she was a member of numerous organizations, including, but not limited to: The Woltz Avenue Block Club, the Every Woman Opportunity Center and the Unity Coalition, a political organization.

Her volunteer services included the American Red Cross, board membership at the Bob Lanier Center for Educational, Physical and Cultural Development, member of the Youth Planning Council and Nurses Aide Task Force of Kaleida. In her commitment to community she organized neighborhood clean-up campaigns and provided help to needy families including a food, clothing and toy distribution project during the holiday seasons and other occasions as needed.

Ms. Ellington is the proud mother of three children and grandmother of four. She worked as a Laboratory Assistant at Kaleida Health (Millard Fillmore Hospital), prior to her election as the Fillmore District Council Member. Ms. Ellington is an active member of Calvary Baptist Church.

Hon. Betty Jean Grant

Betty Jean Grant, a Buffalo City Council member, represented the city's University District. Ms. Grant is also a businesswoman and owner of Grant's Variety Shoppe. She completed a Bachelor of Science Degree at Medaille College and earned a Master of Science Degree from the University at Buffalo.

Ms. Grant is active in numerous community organizations including: The Black Leadership Forum, SCLC, Marcus Garvey Day Committee, the Kwanzaa Committee, the CAO of Erie County; Community Voice Organization, the President's Club and the Black Chamber of Commerce of Western New York. She is the founder of Aids Education, Information Support Services (AEISS) and former president of the Parkridge/Clarence Avenue Block Club. She is a Life Subscribing Member of the NAACP.

She is married to George Grant, and mother of Stacey, Vicki and Sherry Patton, and grandmother of three. She is a member of True Bethel Baptist Church.

Florence D. Johnson

Florence Johnson is a graduate of Buffalo State College and holds a B.S. in Exceptional Education and Elementary Education as well as M.S. in Education. Presently, she serves as project director for Student Support Services at Buffalo State College. In this role, she monitors the academic progress of 200 students who meet the criteria for low income and first generation attending a four-year college. Ms. Johnson recently established a "Summer Bridge Program" specifically designed to help in the retention of first year students at Buffalo State College. Chair of the National Council of Urban Boards of Education, Florence D. Johnson is a member and former president of the City of Buffalo Board of Education. She chairs the strategic planning committee for that board and is its delegate to the Federal Network Advocacy Association. She serves on the Board of Directors of the National School Boards Association and in 1999 served as vice chair of the National Council of Urban Boards of Education.

Listed in Who's Who in American Education, Ms. Johnson is the recipient of numerous awards for her work in education. She has been honored with the Jayne Kadey Award for Teaching Excellence, the Buffalo State College President's Award for Excellence, the New York State Governor's Award for African Americans of Distinction, Omega Psi Phi Fraternity, Edgar A. Love Scholarship Award and the Education Award from the National Conference of Christian and Jews. She was selected to serve on the New York State Commissioner of Education's Advisory Board, and serves on the Council of Great City Schools representing the Buffalo Board of Education.

Ms. Johnson has been an active member of the Calvary Baptist Church for 45 years. During this period she served as Director of Christian Education, teacher of the Sunday School Department, and worked in the Outreach Mission for the EPIC Board to disseminate information to teenage parents on effective parenting. She serves as a member of the Calvary Adult Choir and received the Network of Religious Communities, Inter Religious Ecumenical Award.

Ms. Johnson is married to Mr. George Johnson and has two sons, George, Jr. and Isaac.

Jessica Johnson

A native of Lexington, Kentucky, Jessica (Judy) Grimm was born on June 19,1909. She was the only daughter of Marcellus and Mary Burbridge Grimm. She was an infant when her parents moved to Clifton, Ohio. Mrs. Johnson attended and graduated from the public schools in Clifton. She relocated to Buffalo, New York with her husband Ralph Johnson in 1937.

Described as a pioneer in the political arenas of Buffalo City Hall and New York State Democratic politics, Mrs. Johnson's interest in politics was kindled when she served as the assistant campaign manager for Bishop Ormonde Walker. Bishop Walker campaigned as a Democratic candidate for the Ellicott Council District. In 1957, Mrs. Johnson's friend, Cora P. Maloney, was elected as the first African American female member of the Common Council of Buffalo. Mrs. Johnson served as Mrs. Maloney's secretary. Later, she served as the secretary to Delmar L. Mitchell, a future Common Council President. In 1963, Mrs. Johnson was elected Assistant Secretary of the Democratic State Committee.

In 1966, Mrs. Johnson moved to the executive branch of city government. She served as Director of the License Bureau, the first female to hold that position. Soon after she accepted a position as the confidential aide to then Mayor Frank A. Sedita. Again, she was a first: the first female and the first African American to serve in the Mayor's inner Cabinet. In 1968 Mrs. Johnson edged out, by one vote, Arthur O. Eve now former Deputy Speaker of the New York State Assembly, for election as Chairperson of the 13th Zone Democratic Committee.

She achieved statewide prominence in the Democratic Party hierarchy, in 1973 when she became the Assistant Treasurer of the State Democratic Committee. Three years later, she was elected the First Vice Chairman of that body. She became the first black and first woman to hold the post of state party chairwoman when she assumed the position after the indictment of the then party chairman, Patrick J. Cunningham.

Mayor Stanley M. Makowski appointed her as Buffalo City Treasurer in 1976. She was the first black female to fill this post. In 1977 Mrs. Johnson retired from government service. However, she continued to volunteer in the community, acting as Executive Director of 1490 Enterprises, Inc. for a period of time.

A member of Bethel AME Church since shortly after her move to Buffalo, Mrs. Johnson was a member of the Usher Board, The Walker Willing Workers, Laymen's Association and the Jewletts. She received numerous honors including the Black Achiever's Award in 1975, the Evans-Young Award for community service from the Buffalo Urban League, in 1985 and the Appreciation Award of the Negro Business and Professional Women's Clubs in 1976.

Mrs. Johnson's husband and two sons Jesse and Edward preceded her in death. Her long and productive live ended in September 2003, at the age of 94.

Hon. Barbara Miller-Williams

Barbara Miller-Williams was appointed interim Ellicott District Councilmember by the local Democratic Party Committee members in January 1995. She served as Ellicott District Councilmember for three terms. Prior to her appointment, Ms. Williams served as a Police Officer with the Buffalo Police Department where she was assigned as a D.A.R.E. Officer, Warrant Officer, Police Community Liaison Officer, and Patrol Officer. As a Sergeant First Class in the United States Army Reserve, Ms. Williams is assigned to the 98th Division Second Brigade.

Ms. Williams earned a Secretarial Science Associates Degree and a Bachelor of Science Degree in Office Administration/Criminal Justice. She is a 1998 Buffalo State College graduate with a Masters' Degree in Student Personnel Administration. She is a graduate of Leadership Buffalo '95 and Leadership Buffalo Graduate Program '99. She continues to serve her community as a District Councilmember and is active in the religious and civic communities. She is the parent of two adult daughters and recently became a first time "grandmother."

She has been noted for her leadership and community achievement and is the recipient of numerous Service Awards. She received the Black Achievers in Industry Award, Women for Effective Change Golden Flame Award, Los Tainos Ana Cotton Award, Kappa Alpha Psi Fraternity, Inc. Service Award, 93.7 WBLK Professional of the Month Award, Langston Hughes Cultural Institute Commemorative Award, F. Cecil Brown Democratic Club Award, True Bethel Invisible Soldier Award and the Afro-American Police Leadership Award.

She served on various community boards including the Community Action Organization of Erie County, Inc. and the Buffalo State College Alumni Association. She is a member of Alpha Kappa Alpha Sorority, Inc., Gamma Phi Omega Chapter, Grassroots, Inc., Western New York Hispanics and Friends Civic Association, NAACP, 50 Women with a Vision; Buffalo Urban League, Black Leadership Forum and the New York State Crime Prevention Coalition. She further serves as an Erie County Democratic Committee Member.

Favorite Quote: "I am not a special person. I am a regular person who does special things." Ms. Sarah Vaughan.

Mozella Richardson

A native of Georgia, Mrs. Mozella Richardson moved to Buffalo in the 1940s. She is a graduate of the former Fosdick Masten Park High School. Mrs. Richardson also attended Erie Community College as well as Temple University in Philadelphia, Pa.

Mrs. Richardson is known for her advocacy for parental and community involvement in the educational system. She was always an active member of school PTAs and many other school-related groups. She once stated,

> *For many years I have recognized the important role schools play in the life of the community. I strongly agree with the old adage that "an uneducated and underdeveloped mind is a terrible waste." In an urban setting like Buffalo it is possible to provide various educational options for students and their families to choose from. Therefore, I support a multi-disciplined educational system which affords our students an*

integrated educational experience. However, for any educational program to be successful, parents and educators must be equal partners. To that end I have always been and continue to be a strong advocate for parental involvement in all aspects of their child's education.

Before running for the school board, Mrs. Richardson worked as a teacher's aide. She first was elected to the Board in 1974 as an activist parent. Representing the Central District throughout the course of her tenure, she served four terms as Board President, twice in the early 1980s, once in 1992-1993, and again in 1993-1994. As a Board member, she introduced the idea and design for the School of Music and Performing Arts, suggested the formation of the Board/Community Transportation Committee and the Board/Community Sports Committee. She organized the Central District School Committee and led the discussion at the Board for the change of name of School #39 to the Martin Luther King Community School. In addition, she chaired the Community Advisory Committee for New Construction of the Stanley A. Makowski Early Childhood Center.

Mrs. Richardson retired from the Board in 1995, after 21 years. February 28, 1995 was proclaimed Mozella Richardson Day by then County Executive, Dennis Gorski. Mr. Gorski presented Mrs. Richardson with the Cora P. Maloney Award and an Erie County commemorative plate.

Mrs. Richardson was employed by the Community Action Organization of Erie County, Inc. (CAO) for 25 years. She was Center Manager of the Ellicott CAO Neighborhood Services Center.

She is the recipient of numerous awards and recognitions including: Family of the Year from the Buffalo Branch NAACP, Brotherhood and Sisterhood for Community Service Award from the National Conference for Community and Justice, Community Service Award from the Southern Christian Leadership Conference, Outstanding Service Award from the Community Action Organization of Erie County, Inc. (CAO), Hadji Court Temple #62; Mother of the Year Award and Family Life Award from the Buffalo Urban League.

Mrs. Richardson was married to the late Herbert L. Richardson and together they had ten children.

Uncrowned Queens in Religion

Rev. Natalie P. Alford

The Reverend Dr. Natalie P. Alford is the only child, born in Newark, NJ, to Lawrence and the late Christeen Inez Ellison Alford. Her formative years placed her in Covington, Virginia, Washington, D.C., and Newark and East Orange, New Jersey. She comes from a family that displayed their confession of Christianity in their daily living with affiliation in the African Methodist Episcopal Church (AME). In 1976, she received her Bachelor of Science degree in Management Sciences from Rutgers University, New Jersey.

Reverend Dr. Alford's professional journey is impressive. She has held positions in Prudential Insurance Company's group insurance product in New Jersey and in AT&T Long Lines', second level management, high-risk, high-reward Management Development Program. After divestiture she was recruited by the St. Louis, Missouri based Boise Cascade Consumer Products Division as the Assistant to the Manufacturing Manager. She conducted research that focused on poor managerial female retention. After one year she was promoted to the Administrative Manager for Boise Cascade's largest facility in Orlando, Florida. A merger occurred with Boise Cascade, and Dr. Alford was recruited to fill the Director of Information Services Administration position in the MIS Department for Tupperware Home Parties World Headquarters, Orlando, Florida.

Reverend Dr. Alford began her ministry in 1988, left the corporate environment, and in 1989 enrolled in the Harvard University Divinity School to begin her academic, theological education. While pursing her degree, she was a Director, Summer Camp Enrichment Program, for the St. Matthew AME Church, and Director of an After School Enrichment Program and Elders Minister at Charles Street AME Church in Roxbury, MA. She was ordained an Itinerant Deacon in 1991. After graduating in 1992, she was awarded a President's Administrative Fellowship and was assigned to The Divinity School. She coordinated student programs for the Pan African community, developed programs that bridged the gap between the Office of the Dean and the student community, and provided pastoral presence for the school community. In September 1992, she was ordained an Itinerant Elder, the highest ordination level in the AME Church.

In 1993, after completing the President's Administrative Fellowship, Dr. Alford was recruited to work as the Program Manager for the National Resource Center for the Development of Ethical Leadership from the Black Church Tradition at Colgate Rochester Divinity School/Bexley Hall/Crozer Theological Seminary, Rochester, New York. In December 1994, she was promoted to the position of Director of Program Initiatives. Upon arriving in Rochester, she affiliated with Baber AME Church, became the Assistant to the Pastor, in all capacities: teaching, preaching, developing workshops and counseling both youth and adults. She designed the Sister-to-Sister Ministry for women and girls.

In February 1996, she accepted the Vice President for Program Operations position at the Urban League of Rochester, New York, Inc. In August 1997 she was promoted to Senior Vice President of Operations.

Dr. Alford is an active Lifetime member of Delta Sigma Theta Sorority, Inc., a public service sorority. In August 1997, she was appointed to the position of Regional Associate Chaplain for the Eastern Region for Delta Sigma Theta Sorority, Inc., which encompasses over 150 undergraduate and graduate chapters.

Dr. Alford is an educator and has held many adjunct positions teaching Legal, Ethical, and Crisis Issues in Counseling, Counselor Education, Pastoral Care and Counseling, Loss and Grief, Family and Group Counseling, and Religious Studies and Philosophy at Monroe Community College, University of Rochester, and Colgate Rochester Divinity School, Rochester, New York.

In addition to her profit, not-for-profit, and academic experience, Dr. Alford has held a number of senior level pastoral charges. In November 1995 and 1996, Reverend Alford received her first and second Senior Pastoral charge at St. James AME Church in Utica, New York. In May 1998 and 1999, she received her third and fourth appointment at Bethel AME Church in Lackawanna, NY. She was also appointed a member to the AME Church, Western New York Annual Conference Board of Examiners responsible for training new ministers. In September 1998, Reverend Alford accepted a theological faculty position at The Aquinas Institute of Rochester, New York. From May 2001 to 2003, Reverend Alford received her fifth to eighth pastoral charge as the senior pastor-teacher and first female at Agape AME Church, Buffalo, New York.

In October 1999, from a national search, Reverend Dr. Alford was selected as the Chief Executive Officer for the Girl Scouts of Genesee Valley, Inc. Under her leadership the Council served five diverse, historic and vibrant counties in upstate New York: Genesee, Livingston, Monroe, Orleans and Wyoming counties. She was nstrumental in creating non-traditional Girl Scout collaboration with existing community based organizations and promoted Girl Scouting opportunities cross culturally for "Every Girl, Everywhere."

Reverend Dr. Alford graduated in May 2003, from the University of Rochester, in the Margaret Warner Graduate School of Education and Human Development with a Doctorate of Education in Counseling and Human Development. Her dissertation is titled *Bearing Witness: Inner-city Youth Exposed to Chronic Community Violence.*

Reverend Dr. Alford is the recipient of many prestigious awards. The students, faculty, and administration at The Aquinas Institute of Rochester, New York renamed the St. Monica Club in her honor. This student program is a cultural diversity club, now known as The Natalie Alford Diversity Society. In August 2002, at the International Achievement Awards Banquet, during the Daughters of Elks 100th Anniversary, Reverend Alford received the Emma V. Kelly Award, named after the founder and Supreme Mother of the Daughters of the Improved Benevolent Protective Orders of Elks of the World.

Reverend Dr. Alford is listed in the *African American Who's Who: African American Past and Present, Greater Rochester Area, The New Millennium Edition,* Norex Publications, Rochester, New York, 1998. She has published several articles and is the author of "*Divine Counselor*" published in Sister to Sister: Devotions for and from African American Women[1].

[1] Editor Suzan Johnson Cook, Judson Press, Valley Forge, PA, 1995.

Bertha Hall Amos

Bertha Hall Amos was born on October 5, 1903. She was the eldest of three children born to Washington and Lula Green Hall in Moundville, Alabama. Bertha Hall met and married Harrison Amos in 1921. After he secured employment at the Bethlehem Steel Plant, Bertha and the children left Alabama and relocated to Lackawanna in 1926.The mother of four sons, Archie, Harold, Benjamin and Eli Fletcher, whom she adopted, Mrs. Amos was a pioneer. She was a courageous and God fearing woman who was not only a wife and mother but also a pastor, licensed practical nurse, storekeeper and beautician.

While a member of Second Baptist Church in Lackawanna, she was called to the ministry. During this period, women preachers received little respect and even less recognition. Nonetheless in the 50's, led by the Holy Spirit and the desire to preach from her own pulpit, she purchased the land and built the Pentecostal Faith Baptist Rescue Mission at 64 Steelawanna Avenue. There Pastor Amos preached the unadulterated gospel, married, buried and baptized members of her flock. She served as a pastor at Pentecostal Faith until her health began to fail.

A missionary whose faith was in her work, Pastor Amos was inspired to open a home for the elderly at 818 Humboldt Parkway in Buffalo. Here she cared for the elderly and sick for many years in addition to regularly visiting hospitals and nursing homes. Her work as a woman of God was known and recognized throughout the Western New York area.

Currently she resides in the Episcopal Nursing Home where she continues to minister to others. She characterizes her relationship with the other residents, "These people need me. I brought life to this place." Indeed she does.

Violet Fisher

Reverend Violet Fisher is the second oldest of Deacon William Fisher and Holiness preacher Mrs. Virginia Fisher's five children. Bishop Fisher received two Master's Degrees, one in Education and the other in Divinity, as well as a Doctorate in Divinity. Called to be an evangelist, Bishop Fisher began preaching at the age of 16. Though her roots were in the Methodist Episcopal Church, the opportunity as an African American woman to preach and to be ordained was in the King's Apostle Holiness Church of God. In this movement, she served as National Evangelist and as a short-term missionary to Tanzania, Kenya, Jamaica, Uganda and the Republic of Haiti. In 1969, when her missionary work began in Africa, few African American women were accepted in the mission field, especially in the interior of East Africa. These mission experiences fueled her heart and gave her a passion for foreign work, especially in ministering to women and children. Recently, she and her son, Marcus, helped rebuild the homes of families who had lost everything due to a natural disaster in the Dominican Republic.

In the 1950s when the Bishop received her call to preach and evangelize, African American women did not have the opportunity to support themselves financially as a professional clergyperson. Therefore, during these 20 years, she taught English at the junior high and senior high school levels in the Virginia and Maryland state public school systems.

In 1983, her journey in ministry brought her back to the church of her birth, and in 1988 she was ordained a deacon and in 1990 an elder in the Eastern Pennsylvania Conference of The United Methodist Church. Bishop Fisher served as pastor of St. Daniel's United Methodist Church in Chester, PA, and Sayers Memorial United Methodist Church in Philadelphia. From 1994 to July 2000, she served as district superintendent of the Mary McLeod Bethune District, and during her tenure on the district, was twice appointed dean of the bishop's cabinet.

Endorsed by the Eastern Pennsylvania Conference of The United Methodist Church (UMC), the African American Clergy Women of the UMC, and the UMC Northeastern Jurisdictional Black Methodists for Church Renewal, Violet L. Fisher became the first African American woman to be elected to the episcopacy from the Northeastern Jurisdiction. Reflecting on her consecration in July 2000, Bishop Fisher stated, "This affirmation speaks to all women, especially women of color." Jurisdictional delegates commented after the election:

There is a sense of wonder and delight that a nontraditional leader was elected ... She is a very enthusiastic, energetic people-person with a strong spirit and strong leadership skills ... She knows the pulse of the people ... God anointed her bishop.

Bishop Fisher has general oversight and supervision of approximately 800 local churches and 1500 clergy in the New York West Area. The two annual conferences, North Central New York and Western New York, cover the western, central, and northern sections of New York State, extending from the St. Lawrence Seaway to the Pennsylvania border. As Resident Bishop, she is a trustee of Syracuse University and of Colgate Rochester Crozer Divinity School in Rochester, New York.

Bishop Fisher's awards include the Martin Luther King Freedom Award, Philadelphia Congress Stellar Service Award, National Sojourner Truth Meritorious Award and The United Methodist Church Denman Evangelism Award. She was named Black United Methodist Preacher of the Year for the Eastern Pennsylvania Conference of the United Methodist Church in 1993. Her publications include contributions to *Women of Color Devotional Bible 2000.*

Founder of the Interdenominational World Wide Women Ministers Alliance in 1978 with chapters in the Eastern part of the United States and Bermuda, her other community affiliations include membership in the National Association for the Advancement of Colored People (NAACP), Order of the Eastern Star, Lions Club of America and the Professional Business Women's Association.

Within the structure of The United Methodist Church, she serves on the General Commission on Communication, continues her work with the General Board of Discipleship Committee on Older Adult Ministries and remains a member of National Black Methodists for Church Renewal. In addition, Bishop Fisher represents the Council of

Bishops on the Commission on Pan-Methodist Cooperation and Union. Twice a delegate to the World Methodist Conference, she previously served on the General Board of Church and Society and was Dean of the Northeastern Jurisdiction School of Evangelism.

As Resident Bishop of the New York West Area, Bishop Fisher is called "to serve this present age."

Afterword

The Uncrowned Queens project was inspired by the role that African American women played in the events surrounding the Pan American Exposition of 1901. As we continued our research into the activities of these extraordinary women, we were excited to discover Lena Mason, an uncrowned queen, whose poem on the McKinley Assassination documented the response of African Americans to the assassination and its aftermath. Although she is not a Western New Yorker, Mrs. Mason truly deserves a place in the history that the Uncrowned Queens Institute for Research and Education on Women, Inc. is striving to collect, preserve, and disseminate. We are pleased to share her biography, in addition to her poem, *A Negro Was In It*, with our readers.

....

A Negro Was In It: Lena Mason's[2] poetic response to treatment of James B. Parker, African American Hero in the Assassination of President William McKinley.

The major event that triggered the initial interest in honoring Uncrowned Queens was the City of Buffalo 2001 Centennial celebration of the 1901 Pan American Exposition. In Volume I, specific attention was paid to the Exposition itself and key events during that time. In particular we examined two Midway exhibits, *Darkest Africa and the Old Plantation,* both characterizing people of African descent as either primitive savages or docile, but happy, slaves. During the 1901 Exposition, 8.1 million fairgoers made the Midway the central destination of their visit. We also addressed the role of African American women in responding to the omission of the Negro Exhibit as a more fair representation of people of African descent. In this volume, we focus on an African American male, James B. Parker and his role, often forgotten, during one of the most disturbing events of the Exposition, the assassination of President McKinley.

[2] Special appreciation to Mrs. Ora Anderson Curry who kindly shared Lena Mason's poem and biographical information with the Uncrowned Queens Institute for Research and Education on Women, Inc.

On September 6, 1901, President William McKinley was assassinated while attending the Pan American Exposition. Blacks reacted to the President's death with the same horror, anger and sadness as other Americans. But they also had reason to feel pride because one of their own played a heroic role in this tragic event. James B. Parker, who was in line to shake hands with McKinley during his visit at the Temple of Music, was the first to grab Leon Czolgosz, the assassin following the shooting of the President. Parker was credited with preventing the firing of a third, immediately fatal, shot at McKinley.

Parker, a waiter in one of the Midway restaurants, was promptly praised for saving the President's life. According to Daryl Rasuli, Parker was "besieged by souvenir hunters" who wanted to buy buttons and other pieces of his clothing immediately after his heroic act.[3] Parker was even inducted into the all white fraternal organization, the Don't Knock Society."[4] Yet as quickly as he was acclaimed for his great deed, Parker's veracity came under fire. Members of the President's Secret Service as well as a prominent Buffalo citizen accused him of making false claims. James Quakenbush, a well-known Buffalo attorney, claimed that he was an eyewitness to the shooting and did not see James Parker subdue the assassin. Quakenbush was called to testify at the trial of Leon Czolgosz, but James Parker was never called as a witness.

Black Buffalonians were incensed by the attempts to discredit Parker. On September 27th a protest meeting was held at the Vine Street African Methodist Church. During the meeting, a five-member committee was appointed to examine Parker's account of the story. As the committee met privately, Parker arrived at the church. However, according to reports of the time, he refused to publicly address the crowd. Following their deliberations, the committee issued a resolution that stated that the colored citizens regretted the "clash of statement" regarding Parker's role in foiling the gunmen's attempt to fire a third time, but believed that the evidence supported Parker's version of the events.[5]

---

[3] Rasuli, Daryl. "James B. Parker Revisited." *Western New York Heritage Magazine,* Vol. 5, No. 1, Winter 2002, pp.22-23.

[4] "Parker is a Don't knock: Big Negro who acted quickly at shooting of President is a member" Courier, September, 1901.

[5] "Negros laud Parker: Ask history to give him credit they think is due. "Express, September 27, 1901.

Parker was not from Buffalo. In fact, he had only recently arrived and his stint as a waiter was a temporary job. He was scheduled to start a new job, in November 1901, as a "traveling agent" for the Gazetteer and Guide.[6] The periodical's publisher/editor, James A. Ross, a staunch Parker supporter, took up the cause. He wrote a letter to the Editor of the Buffalo Express, dated September 26, 1901, that decried the attacks on Parker's credibility.

Ross said that he and Parker's attorney, Mr. Thomas, had contacted the District Attorney, "the Honorable Mr. Penney," and expressed concern that Parker was not called as a witness at the assassin's trial. The letter further stated, "I also stated to Parker when his claim was disputed that I thought he should make an affidavit as to the correctness of his statement, but others stated this was unnecessary. I then insisted that it should be done and if it was proven that it was incorrect there should be but one alternative and that was to go over the Niagara Falls."[7] In addition to his fervent support of James Parker, Mr. Ross, it seems, also had a sense of humor.

In further defense of Parker, Ross quoted a news article from the Brockton Times, Brockton, Massachusetts. The article provided an eyewitness statement that confirmed the contention that Parker should have received the credit for being "the first man to land on the assassin." Ross concluded his letter by stating that "others concurring with this statement can be shown from those who are disinterested parties."[8]

In spite of the Black community's efforts the movement to discredit Parker gained momentum. A retraction of support for Parker was printed by one local newspaper. Under the banner, "The Case of J.B. Parker," the paper blamed its failure to check and confirm its sources, and the testimony of James Quakenbush, as leading to the reversal of its support for Parker. The paper admonished Black citizens to drop the issue as it was not one of "race prejudice, but of the simple facts in the premises. These facts are of record and Mr.

---

[6] Op. Cit. Rasuli, p.22

[7] Ross, James. "Parker's Claims" Letter to Editor Buffalo Express, September 26,1901

[8] Ibid.

Parker and his well-meaning friends are invited to inspect and calmly consider them before they utter rash accusations...."[9]

With his claims thoroughly dismissed, it appears that James Parker faded out of history as quickly as he was thrust into it. Nothing else has been found regarding his activities or residence following the meeting at the Vine Street Church. However, African Americans through out the country viewed the treatment of Parker as an injustice and a blow to race pride and some continued to advocate on his behalf. The incident elicited a response from an Uncrowned Queen of her time, Evangelist Lena Mason.

Mrs. Lena Mason[10] *(pictured left)* was born in Quincy, Illinois on May 8, 1864. She attended the Douglass High School of Hannibal, Missouri and furthered her education at Professor Knott's School in Chicago. Mrs. Mason entered the ministry at the age of 23. During the first three years of her ministry she preached to whites exclusively. Later her congregations were mixed. She was a member of the Colored Conference. It was noted that she had preached in nearly every state in the nation. She was lauded for her speaking ability and it was said "the preachers are few who can excel her in preaching."

A contemporary, Rev. C.L. Leonard, pastor of the Central German M. E. Church, said of her, "I desire to express my highest appreciation of Mrs. Mason's church and effective evangelical work in my church and in many others. Mrs. Mason is now making a tour of the South, and by her lectures and sermons is doing a work among the colored people that will bear good fruit in the future. One only needs to hear Mrs. Mason lecture and preach to understand how it is that one never tires listening to her."

In addition to her ministry, Mrs. Mason was a poet and songwriter. She authored the poem A Negro In It; clearly an "ode" to James B. Parker and an admonition to those who sought to deny him appropriate recognition for his actions in the assassination of

[9] Donelson, james Edura. "Death and burial of President William McKinley," Scrapbook, undated., Buffalo Erie County Public Library.

[10] Photo courtesy of The African American Registry, http://www.aaregistry.com.

President William McKinley. Lena Mason's work and her recognition of James Parker is representative of only one African American woman who was devoted to ensuring that the accomplishments of at least one Uncrowned King would not remain unheralded.
We are indebted to Ms. Mason for her work.

Barbara A. Seals Nevergold, Ph.D.
Co-Founder
Uncrowned Queens Institute for
Research and Education on Women, Inc.

A Negro In It[11]
by Lena Mason

In the last civil war,
The white folks, they began it,
But before it could close,
The Negro had to be in it.

At the battle of San Juan Hill,
The rough-riders they began it;
But before victory could be won
The Negro had to be in it.

The Negro shot the Spaniard from the tree,
And never did regret it;
The rough-riders would have been dead today
Had the Negro not been in it.

To Buffalo, McKinley went,
To welcome people in it;
The prayer was prayed, the speech made,
The Negro, he was in it.

September sixth, in Music Hall,
With thousands, thousands in it,
McKinley fell, from the assassin's ball,
And the Negro, he got in it.

He knocked the murderer to the floor,
He struck his nose, the blood did flow;
He held him fast, all nearby saw,
When for the right, the Negro in it.

J.B. Parker is his name,
He from the state of Georgia came;
He worked in Buffalo, for his bread,
And there he saw McKinley dead.

---

[11] Exerted from the *Bapbtist Hymnal*, Philadelphia, American Bapbtist Publication Society, 1903.

They bought his clothes for souvenirs,
And may they ever tell it,
That when the President was shot
A brave Negro was in it.

He saved him from the third ball,
That would have taken life with it;
He held the foreigner fast and tight,
The Negro sure was in it.

McKinley now in heaven rests,
Where he will ne'er regret it;
And well he knows, that in all his joys
There was a Negro in it.

White man, stop lynching and burning
This black race, trying to thin it,
for if you go to heaven or hell
You will find some Negroes in it.

Parker knocked the assassin down,
And to beat him, he began it;
In order to save the President's life,
Yes, the Negro truly was in it.

You may try to shut the Negro out,
The courts, they have begun it;
But when we meet at the judgment bar
God will tell you the Negro is in it.

Pay them to swear a lie in court,
Both whites and blacks will do it;
Truth will shine, to the end of time,
And you will find the Negro in it.

Update on the Uncrowned Queens Institute for Research and Education on Women, Inc.

Since the publication of Volume I of Uncrowned Queens: African American Women Community Builders of Western New York, several key events have occurred including securing Not-for-Profit status for the Uncrowned Queens Institute for Research and Education on Women, Inc., and identification of a Board of Directors. Other activities include changes to the home page of the award winning home web site, http://wings.buffalo.edu/uncrownedqueens e.g., a regional map was added depicting the growth of the project to other areas of Western New York including Rochester, Albany, Niagara Falls, Depew and Lackawanna. Numerous biographies were also added to the site and continue to reflect the diversity of African American women who continue to build the Western New York community. And, true to the original goals of the project, this volume includes the biographies of a number of women whose activities date from the early 20th century.

Support for the Uncrowned Queens Institute continues and the friends, families as well as the Uncrowned Queens themselves continue to devise new and innovative ways to utilize the Web site, including downloading bios to view at birthday celebrations, family reunions and "going home" celebrations. Students at various levels, e.g., high school to college, utilize the site to conduct research on the Uncrowned Queens. Biographical sketches were downloaded and used for employment applications, nominations for community boards, award ceremonies and obituaries. Others used the site to begin research on family history. Still others utilized the site to update information on themselves, friends and family members. Many inquiries about establishing Uncrowned Queens' chapters in other states were received from both men and women from California, Illinois, Maryland, Michigan, New Jersey, and Pennsylvania.

One of the major goals of the Uncrowned Queens Institute continues to be the export of the Uncrowned Queens model throughout the nation. Consistent with this goal, the Uncrowned Queens model is being replicated in the State of Oklahoma. In 2003, the Oklahoma Capitol Complex and Centennial Commemoration

Commission placed the Uncrowned Queens project on the Master Plan identifying the project as an official Oklahoma Centennial Commission project and citing that "...the project will reach out to communities of all sizes and that it will create archives that will be invaluable to students, scholars and the public." The Oklahoma Web site will represent women from seventy-two counties and will be hosted by Langston University, a historical black college/university (HSBC).

About the Authors

Peggy Brooks-Bertram (pictured on the left side of the photograph) is a native of Baltimore, Maryland. She received a B.A. from Goucher College, a MPH and a Dr. P.H. from The Johns Hopkins University School of Hygiene and Public Health. In 2002, she received a second doctorate (Ph.D.) in American Studies at the University at Buffalo. She is an Adjunct Professor in African American Studies at the University of Buffalo and teaches in the Department of Social and Preventive Medicine at the University at Buffalo School of Public Health.

Dr. Bertram is the co-founder of the Uncrowned Queens Institute for Research and Education on Women, Inc. and President of the Board. She is also CEO of Jehudi Educational Services, an independent consultant firm specializing in K-12 curriculum development, staff training and development, research and program evaluation, and conference/seminar planning. She has authored two book chapters on depression, including "Social and Psychological Aspects of Women's Health: A Diversified Perspective" in *Psychiatric Issues in Women* (U. Halbreich, Editor, 1997) and "African American Women: Disfigured Images in the Epidemiology of Depression" in *African American Women and Health* (Catherine Collins, Editor, 1997). She is also an independent scholar in African American women's history and well-known lecturer on the life and writings of Drusilla Dunjee Houston. She will be a contributing a chapter on Drusilla Dunjee Houston for the new edition of *Black Women in America: An Historical Encyclopedia,* edited by Professor Darlene Clark Hine.

Dr. Bertram was also a columnist with *The Buffalo Challenger* and is author of numerous editorials on the Buffalo Board of Education and other related topics appearing in *The Buffalo Challenger* from 1989 to 1995. She is also a consultant on the William Still Family Underground Railroad Project and is author of numerous unpublished books including *Drusilla Dunjee Houston: Historical Oversight; Rev. John William Dunjee and William Still: Selling the*

Underground Railroad and *Africa on My Stairs* a five-part children's book, as well as numerous poems on ancient Africa.

Dr. Bertram is also a member of the Board of Directors of the Buffalo and Erie County Historical Society and Chair of the St. John Baptist Church Hospice Development Committee.

Barbara A. Seals Nevergold *(pictured right, p. 158)* received a B.S. degree in French Education from Buffalo State College and an M.ED. and Ph.D. in counseling education from the University at Buffalo. Currently, Dr. Nevergold is the Director of Student Support Services at the University of Buffalo's Educational Opportunity Center. She is also an instructor at Empire State College where she teaches courses in Domestic Violence, Counseling, Family Therapy, Cultural Diversity, Child Welfare and Human Service Delivery Systems.

She has authored several published articles including: *Doing the Pan: the African American Experience at the 1901 Pan American Exposition in Afro-Americans in New York Life and History* (January 2004 publication date); *Fantastic Color and Special Effects: The Seals Ebony Studio* in the Spring 2002 edition of the *Western New York Heritage Magazine; To Be an Instrument for Their Voices: Finding, Writing and Sharing Family Histories in Afro-Americans in New York Life and History,* Vol. 25, No. 2, July 2001; and *Transracial Adoption: In the Child's Best Interest? in African America Women's Health and Social Issues,* Catherine F. Collins (editor). Dr. Nevergold is doing research for a book on the history of African Americans in Buffalo, New York during the post World War II era. The book will use photographs taken by her father, the late Rev. Seals, during his 45-year career as a photographer in Buffalo's black community.

Dr. Nevergold is the co-founder of the Uncrowned Queens Institute for Research and Education on Women, Inc. and Treasurer of the Board. Dr. Nevergold is a member of Alpha Kappa Alpha Sorority, Inc., Xi Epsilon Omega Chapter, and the Erie County Chapter of The Links, Incorporated. She also is active in the Rotary Club of Buffalo and serves on boards of the Buffalo Psychiatric Center, Heritage Centers, Studio Arena Theater and the Christian Education Ministry at her church, St. John Baptist.

Since the inauguration of the Uncrowned Queens Project, Drs. Nevergold and Bertram have received numerous joint honors including the Williams Wells Brown Award from the Afro-American Historical Association of the Niagara Frontier, for their efforts to chronicle and preserve local African American history. In 2001, they received the University at Buffalo Star Award for outstanding work on the Pan-American Exposition Centennial celebration. They have received other awards from women's organizations in Buffalo including Xi Epsilon Omega Chapter of Alpha Kappa Alpha Sorority Inc.'s Excellence in Education Award, The Mary B. Talbert Civic and Cultural Club's President's Award for Community Service, and the Women of Excellence Award from Gamma Phi Omega Chapter of Alpha Kappa Alpha Sorority, Inc. Further, the Buffalo Urban League honored Drs. Bertram and Nevergold with the 2002 Community Service Award.

Drs. Nevergold and Bertram also co-author *African, Darkies and Negroes: Black Faces at the Pan American Exposition of 1901* (in press), a book on the history of African and African American involvement in the Pan American Exposition of 1901. They will also share their story of the development of the Uncrowned Queens Project in an upcoming article. Their goal with the Uncrowned Queens Institute continues to be exporting the Uncrowned Queens model national-wide in order to build a network of Uncrowned Queens.

Index

B

E

F

G

L

M

N

O

P

R

S

X

Y

Z